The Rejuvenation of the Soul

Also by Fode Drame

The Splendors of Quran: English Translation of the Quran
Expansions Volume 1: The Purpose of Creation
Expansions Volume 2: The Way is Peace
Expansions Volume 3: The Awakening
Expansions Volume 5: The 99 Names of Allah

Websites
www.expansions.ca
www.zawiyah.ca

Videos
www.youtube.com/zawiyahfoundation

EXPANSIONS VOLUME 4

The Rejuvenation of the Soul

Fode Drame

Tasleem Publications
Vancouver, Canada

TASLEEM PUBLICATIONS
www.expansions.ca
The Rejuvenation of the Soul
EXPANSIONS - VOLUME FOUR

I. Spirituality
II. Personal Development

Contents

NOTE ON THE ARABIC CONTENT

The content of this work is intended for a general audience which may not be familiar with the Arabic language or Islamic spirituality. This is why the author preferred to use the English equivalent for most key Arabic terms. In the few cases where there was no true English equal, then the Arabic word was kept and transliterated into its simplest readable format and left italicized for clear recognition (e.g. *taqwa*).

The exception to this italicization of Arabic is the usage of the following proper names:

Allah – God's proper name.

Iblis – comes from the Arabic word *balasa*, which means to lose hope. Iblis is actually the one who lost hope in God. His name is pivotal to understanding his role in Islamic spirituality and mysticism and cannot be overlooked.

Hajj – the Muslim's pilgrimage to Mecca and the rituals relating to this fifth pillar of Islam.

PART I

DEFINITION OF THE HEART

CHAPTER 1

Expansion and the Heart

A heart is the core of any entity. In which case, not only humans possess a heart but all entities in the universe have a claim to a heart. For that matter, a mountain has a heart, which means the core of that mountain. A tree has a heart, which means the core of that tree. The earth has a heart, which means the core of the earth. The heavenly firmament has a heart, which means the core thereof. Each animals has a heart, which means the core and the essential structure of that animal. Plants possess a heart, which means the essential core of that plant. There is not a being or an entity in our cosmos that does not have a claim to a heart.

The formation of any entity begins with its heart. Then, from the heart the other levels of its structure are developed. For example, for a mountain, its foundation is its heart—its core—from which the rest of its structure expanded and grew. Similarly the earth, it was from the core or the heart of the earth that its creation began and from there the rest of its structure grew, developed and expanded. The same principle goes for the heavens, the animals, plants, and humans.

As long as the core of an entity remains alive and active, that particular entity will continue to grow, develop, and expand. If the heart of an entity ceases to be active and alive, then its growth, development, and expansion ceases as well. The health of the entire structure of an entity depends on the health of its core, known as the heart. If the heart ails, the entire structure ails. If the heart lives, the entire structure lives. If the heart decays, the entire structure decays and falls apart because the core, or the heart, has ceased to have any more potential to grow and develop. For anything that is not growing will necessarily be decaying. It is in this respect we understand the growth of an entity, its expansion and extinction. Life is a continued process of growth and expansion, and death is the contrary to that; death is contraction, constriction, and decrease. There is no middle way between the two. Either you increase or you decrease. This is why we see individuals increase from their birth and suddenly begin to decrease ending in a total demise. In the same way we understand the rise and the fall of nations, powers, systems of belief, and systems of faith. As well as languages, races, ethnicities and the breed of an animal, etc.

This law applies to all levels of existence, from the slightest to the mightiest. Their ability to continue to live depends on the health and the potential of their core to grow and expand. Referring the this phenomena, the Prophet, peace be upon him, said:

> There is a small piece in the body, if that piece remains healthy, the whole body remains healthy, and if that piece gets corrupted, the entire body gets corrupted. That small piece is the heart. (*Sahih Bukhari*)

This prophetic tradition comments on a verse in the Quran:

> And the heaven, We built it with power and verily We certainly are expanding it. And the earth, We rolled it out and how best are those who spread out [the earth]. (Chapter *The Scatterers*, 51:47-48)

These two verses are telling us that the firmament was developed from a nucleus and that God continues to expand it.

And that the earth as well was developed from a tiny nucleus and that God continues to expand it as well. The earth and the heaven have not stopped expanding since the beginning of their creation. And they will only cease to expand when they have reached to their outermost limit. For when the heavens cannot expand anymore, they will collapse. And when the earth cannot expand anymore, it is bound to fall apart. It is the law of God, and to the law of God no exception exists. Similarly, when a human being reaches the outermost limit of expansion, he or she dies. And when a plant reaches its outermost expansion, it dies. When a mountain reaches its outermost expansion, it falls apart. When an animal reaches its outermost expansion, it dies. In the same way, one day the earth and the heavenly firmament will cease to be. They will reach their outermost limit of expansion. When they cannot expand anymore, they will start to contract and constrict, leading them to their demise.

Instead of moving outward farther and farther away from each other, they will begin to move inward, closer and closer to each other, ending in a final collision between the different parts of our cosmos. This is called the reunion of the pairs. The earth and the heaven will collide together. The moon and the sun will collide and merge into each other. The east and the west, the high and low, the heavenly ocean and earthly ocean, the night and the day: everything will merge into an infinite unity.

This infinite unity was at the beginning, before they emerged out of the *noon*-ن (consonant n). The *noon* is the primordial water, the ocean of unity and indifferentiation. This is the ocean of annihilation (*fana*), God says:

> Everyone thereupon will come to an end (*fana*). But will abide the face of your Lord. Master of the majesty and of the grace. (The Quran, chapter *The All Merciful,* 55:26-27)

Following this absolute immersion and annihilation of the entire creation into the dark water of the beginning and the waves of nothingness, a re-emergence of the creation will take place.

That re-emergence is called the day of resurrection, followed by the day of reckoning *(yawm al qiyama)*. The question that imposes itself at this junction is whether there is any escape and alternative route to avoid this universal collision and this cosmic annihilation? The answer is yes, there is an alternative route and a "sauf conduit" out of this universal chaos. Yes, it is avoidable. Yes, there is an exception to it. And yes, there are those who are exempted from its furor and terror. That route is the path of enlightenment of a second birth, the enlightened birth, before the physical death.

The one who has attained enlightenment, has been born again while alive and not to fare a second birth, they are exempted from the process of resurrection. They have already passed the test and they are set away, seated under the shade of the throne of the Almighty; while the remaining unenlightened, and therefore unborn ones, are tossed back and forth by the waves of the ocean of annihilation. It evokes the image of the ark of Noah on the ocean. Noah's ark is an analogy of the throne of God. Those in the ark along with Noah are the enlightened ones, and will not be swallowed again by the water, nor will they be subjected anymore to the rigors of rebirth. They navigate in peace and tranquility, in joy, in buoyancy, in the company of the Almighty, their beloved One.

The crew of that ark are the Prophets: Adam, Noah (Nuh), Abraham (Ibrahim), Joseph (Yusuf), Moses (Musa), Jesus ('Isa), and Muhammad, peace be upon them all. And the passengers are the enlightened ones, the saints, who had experienced their individual absolute expansion while they still lived on earth, rubbing shoulders with their human fellows. To their human fellows, they appear to be the same individuals they once knew, who would eat, drink, and socialize with them. There is no outward visible change in their physical appearances, but inwardly they were a new people. They are enlightened beings; they are light beings who are born spiritually again, grown internally and blossomed. But their outer bodies remain as shells that veil and hide their new selves from the vain eyes of their fellow humans. When the body—or the shell—of the englightened one reaches its outermost limit, it will break through and merge into the light and join the glorious ones that are stationed around the throne of the Almighty.

They merge out of their shells like a chick breaks through its egg. The egg is nothing but an outer cover for the chick inside. Similarly, the body is for the light being inside. They do not fear the rigors of a second creation and are not subjected to the cycle of growth and decay any longer. They have joined the divine ship that journeys on the water. For those who fell short of boarding onto this ship, they are bound to be swallowed by the water again. They are bound to undergo the horrors of re-creation. They neither live a real life, nor do they die a complete death. As God says:

> And those who disbelieve, for them will be the fire of hell. They are not overwhelmed by it so that they die nor its punishment made light upon them. Thus do We reward anyone who is ungrateful. (The Quran, chapter *Originator of Creation,* 35:36)

This is a statement of the cycle of growth and decay, and decay and growth, or neither growth nor decay. This is what the concept of hell represents. It's a place whereby the inhabitants neither live a real life, nor are they subjected to a complete death. Rather, they are allowed to have a taste of life followed by a taste of death as a representation of the cycle of growth and death. As for those who enter heaven, they enjoy a full measure of life, which is different from a taste of life. They are not subjected to any taste of death, not the faintest form of it. Rather, they are in a continual and eternal growth and expansion, this time, forever.

We can picture two human beings living on earth; one of them is already living a life of heaven, for he is in a state of continual growth and expansion. And the other is living the life of hell for he is in a continual growth and decay. This one grows a moment and decays another, grows a day then decays a day after. His growth is not steady, nor forthcoming. So, the life of heaven and the life of hell begin here on earth. And the decision is yours to make.

CHAPTER 2

Expansion and Our Universe

At the beginning, our universe was a tiny spec in the horizon, which began to expand under the influence of the infusion of the spirit of God. As it expanded and grew, it multiplied, spawning the different entities that make up our cosmos. The earth developed and the firmament developed above it as a roof. The stars were spawned in great numbers. The sun and the moon divided into two from one cell. In this way pairs were developed and with each new infusion of divine breath our universe underwent a new expansion.

This continued until the point where the first human was created. It is at this point that our cosmos experienced a degree of expansion as never before. This is the special contribution brought to the development of our universe by the human being, the chosen one of God. This first human being was at the same time a man, a prophet, and a messenger; which means that he was someone who had been infused with the Holy Spirit. This entailed an even greater expansion of our universe than in normal circumstances of its expansion. The universe then continued to expand with the coming of the successive messengers due to the infusions of divine breath, called the Holy Spirit (*rooh-ul-quds*). This extraordinary blowing of a new spirit is the divine breath of the Almighty Allah into the body of the universe.

Since that breath is ongoing, our universe as well has to carry on expanding to accommodate the new volume of breath infused into it. This phenomenon is a daily occurrence. Every-day, the Almighty makes his presence into the first heaven and blows His spirit into the body of the universe in the last third of the night.

> He pronounces the commandment from the heaven down to the earth then it rises up to Him in a day, which is worth thousand years from that you count. (The Quran, chapter *The Prostration*, 32:5)

The term "commandment" in this verse, refers to the Holy Breath of the Almighty. For His breath is His word. And His word is His speech. And His speech is His commandment. So when we say He commands someone, it means that He infused that person with His spirit. So God's speaking to His messengers is as good as saying God is inspiring them, as it is explained in the Quran:

> And it is not fitting for a human being that Allah should speak to him directly except as an inspiration or from behind a veil or that he sends a messenger to inspire by His leave what He pleases. Verily He is, All-High All-Wise. (Chapter *The Consultation*, 42:51)

"An inspiration" refers mainly to the mode of communication God adopted with Jesus, peace be upon him. "From behind a veil" refers to how God communicated with Moses, peace be upon him. And "sends a messenger" refers to the angel Gabriel that God sent to communicate with Muhammad, peace be upon him.

> And thus We have inspired unto you a spirit from Our commandment. You never knew before what was the book or what was the faith but We have made it a light

> We guide by it whom We please from Our servants and verily you do guide to a path most upright. (Chapter *The Consultation*, 42:52)

We deduce from the foregoing verses that God's speaking to a man amounts to God infusing him with the Holy Spirit.

> Exalted is He in ranks, Master of the throne, He sends down spirit from His commandment upon anyone He pleases from among His slaves so that He may warn of the day of the encounter. (The Quran, chapter *The Forgiver*, 40:15)

In light of the foregoing, we understand that God sends down His word of command, meaning His spirit is blown into our universe, and that accordingly, there is a new expansion every day in our universal system, but most humans are unaware of it. Human beings are distracted in their pursuit of vain pleasures and the fantasies of their imagination. As for those who possess a living heart, they are indeed conscious of this daily commandment of God, and the corresponding expansion that our universe experiences, for their hearts also experience this expansion. However, these daily expansions of our universe are comparatively minor to the epoc-making expansions that take place with the advent of a messenger into our cosmic system. In this case, not only one word of commandment is released, but many words, signifying a greater amount of inspiration released into the body of our cosmic system, by virtue of the new patron of the universe. His heart receives the revelation of these words and as his heart expands, our universe expands with it.

This extraordinary expansion does not take place without consequences in the system of our universe because it entails broadening the boundaries of the universe. It entails stretching the limits of our universe as it stretches itself. The analogy of this stretching is the labors of childbirth; before our universe can adjust itself to the new limits it has been forced to accommodate itself to. This is why natural calamities abound during these periods of cosmic restructuration. Stars fall off in great numbers. Oceans burst their banks. Mountains bulge, emitting fire and sulphur. And humans engage in wars and bloodshed, for everyone is affected by this new expansion. Until finally, when the adjustment is completed, a new order is born. This was the case at the time of Adam, and at the time of Noah, peace be upon them both. Of course the flood and the ark is a testament to that. It was the case at the time of Abraham and at the time of Moses, peace be upon them; the nine plagues in Egypt, the opening up of the ocean, the water springing up from the bowels of rocks, are testimony to that. At the time of Jesus, peace be upon him, the wars before and after the Roman Empire pitted against others. At the time of Prophet Muhammad, peace be upon him, the breaking of stars and their falling in great numbers, all pointed to the new labor pains under which our universe was going.

It is narrated that during the time of the Prophet Muhammad, Iblis sent his armies abroad to wreak havoc in the universe. They came back complaining to him that they were unable to get close to the heavens for being constantly pelted with stars and they did not know the reason thereof. Iblis said to them, go around and look in the earth, something unusual must have happened. They went around exploring the different parts of the earth till they came upon the Prophet and his companions praying in one of the valleys of Mecca. And when they reported back to him, he said, "Yes, this is the reason why stars are falling in great numbers." Another testimony to that is the splitting of the moon. Not only did the moon split in this circumstance, indicating its expansion to new limits, but the sun must have undergone the same cracking and opening up to new limits, and the stars falling signifies their expansion and explosion. For if they failed to crack, open up, and expand, there would have been no moon today, nor will there have been a sun. In this manner we witness the birth of a new universe. With every message a new sun is born, a new moon, a new heaven, and a new earth. For they have all expanded and they have all completed their labor and they are all reborn again. Likewise, many animals, plants, mountains, and many humans also expand to keep up with the new stretching of the limits. But there are also many who perish. Those who are incapable of keeping up with the new expansion either lack elasticity, suppleness, and flexibility in their hearts or are restive to growth and expansion.

CHAPTER 3

Expansion and the Increase of Knowledge

Knowledge is the definition of the nature and the count of proportions between different parts of a whole. That is to say, the basis and the foundation of all knowledge is computation and numbers, as well as measurement; in summary, it is calculation and mathematics. All knowledge is about proportions and relationships. Being the case, we expect that with each considerable expansion of our universe there will be a corresponding increase in knowledge. That is to say, a new task to redefine the new limits, the new boundaries, the new proportions, and the new relationships between the individual members of our cosmos. For example, the sun and the moon, during the earlier era of the universe, had a proportion of 1 to 1,000. If the sun expands anew and the moon expands anew, then definitely this proportion of 1 to 1,000 cannot apply anymore. The new proportion has to be defined, for example, it may have increased to 20 to 20,000. This applies to other relationships that exist between the various members of our cosmic system. There is a new knowledge that comes into existence that contains the former and surpasses it. If we hold on to the former and disregard the present new knowledge just born, then we are resisting the new order set in place by the Maker, the Almighty, and following the new expansion and the new spirit that masterminds it.

This does not mean that the knowledge established in the earlier era was erroneous. On the contrary, it was correct and valid, but only as far as that era lasted because it will not be able to explain the new relationships in the existing order. The music of the cosmos has changed and the old dance has been outstripped. Not to dance according to the new tune will mean to be left behind by the new train.

It is in this manner and in this context that we can understand the revelation of successive books of law revealed to successive messengers. The new message of the new era contains more information than the old message of the earlier era. Again, we stress that the new one does not invalidate the earlier. Rather, it expands it to new realities that did not exist earlier. For there is no contradiction in the word of God, nor in the message of God. It is one and the same. However, the spirit keeps on expanding and the knowledge keeps on increasing.

The knowledge brought to Adam, peace be upon him, the law of Adam, and the book of Adam got expanded to new limits with the coming of Noah, peace be upon him. The law of Noah and the knowledge brought by Noah got expanded to new limits with the advent of Abraham, peace be upon him. The law of Abraham and the knowledge revealed onto him got expanded to new limits with the message of Moses, peace be upon him. The law of Moses and the message revealed onto him got expanded to new limits with the advent of Jesus, peace be upon him. The law of Jesus and the knowledge revealed onto him got expanded and broadened to new limits with the coming of the seal of Prophethood, Muhammad, peace be upon him. God says:

> We have indeed sent down the Torah, in it there is guidance and light. The prophets who submitted themselves to Allah deliver judgment through it for those who adhere to Judaism and so do the rabbis and the sages be-

> cause of what they were entrusted from the book of Allah and they were witnesses over it. Therefore do not defer to men but defer to Me and do not sell My signs for a trifling price and whoever does not judge by that which Allah has sent, then they are the ones who are the disbelievers. And We have written therein upon them that the life is for the life and the eye is for the eye and the nose is for the nose and the ear is for the ear and the tooth is for the tooth and the wounds by retribution. But whoever forgoes it as a charity, then that is an absolution for it and whoever does not judge by that which Allah has sent down, then they are the ones who have wronged their souls. And in their wake We sent Jesus son of Mary testifying to that which went before him, from the Torah, and We gave him the Gospel; in it there is a guidance and a light testifying to that which went before it from the Torah, and a guidance and an admonition for those who guard their own souls. So let the people of the Gospel deliver their judgment through that which Allah has sent down in it and whoever does not judge by that which Allah has sent down, then those are the ones who are renegades. Then We sent unto you the book by the truth testifying to the books which went before it and superseding above it. Therefore judge between them by that which Allah has sent down and do not follow their vain desires departing from that which has come to you from the truth. For each one of you We have appointed a law and a way and had Allah so willed, He certainly would have made you one nation but it is that He may try you through that which He has given you, therefore vie with one another in the good things and unto Allah is your place of returning all together. And then He will inform you about all that wherein you used to disagree. (The Quran, chapter *The Heavenly Food Bowl*, 5:44-48)

This expansion in the laws of God is not random, nor is it arbitrary, but instead it is well informed and calculated. Essentially, the expansion in the laws of God has to be because every new expansion, as we said earlier, will require a new definition of new limits, of new boundaries, of new proportions and relationships that have taken place in our cosmos. In essence, the Divine Law is a cosmic law, and a universal law. But, since our universe does not stop increasing, the laws of our universe cannot stop increasing. Therefore, all old laws are surpassed by new ones.

For example, someone living in the era of Noah, peace be upon him, and wanting to hold on to the law of Adam, peace be upon him, would only condemn himself and would not keep up with the new light sent down by God. Rather, he would be in darkness because the former compared to the latter is like darkness compared to light. The former constitutes a contraction as opposed to the new, the present, which constitutes an expansion. In the same way, someone living in the era of Abraham, peace be upon him, and wanting to hold the earlier law of Noah, would most certainly be outrun by the divine train. And so the one who lived in the era of Moses, peace be upon him, and refused to adhere to the law of Moses would most certainly be left behind. And so the one who lived in the era of Jesus, peace be upon him, and did not embrace the teachings and the light brought by Jesus would most certainly not fit in the new order brought by the new expansion of our universe. Finally, the one who lives in the era of Muhammad, peace be upon him, and does not comply with the teachings and the guidance of Muhammad will most certainly be left in the dark. That is the law of God. That is the Justice of God. That is the system of God, and there is no exception to it. Refer to the above verses in *The Heavenly Food Bowl* (5:44-48).

Now we see that every new expansion brings an enriched body of knowledge and expands on the one that was existing earlier. It is because of this enrichment of the sources that there is a greater degree of sophistication in the relationships between parts of the cosmos, and at the same time a greater simplification and clarification of knowledge. The more light there is, the more simple the truth becomes. In that respect, we see that the divine, or the cosmic laws revealed successively from Adam, down to Prophet Muhammad, peace be upon him, with a greater degree of simplification and at the same time of sophistication. The more the universe expands, the more light comes into it. Correspondingly, the more the knowledge expands, the more light comes into it. Thereby it becomes increasingly simpler, more flexible, more supple, more resilient, less cumbersome and less burdensome.

> Those who follow the messenger, the unlettered prophet, whom they find written with them in the Torah and in the Gospel. He commands them to the kind things and he forbids them from the wicked things and he makes clean things lawful for them and he makes the unclean things unlawful for them and he takes away their heavy burdens from them as well as the fetters which were upon them. As for those who believe in him, and honor him, and help him and follow the light which was sent down with him, it is they who will prosper. Say, 'O you mankind! Verily I am the messenger of Allah to you, all together; He, for whom is the dominion of the heavens and of the earth. There is no deity save He. It is He who gives life and puts to death.' Therefore believe in Allah and in His messenger, the unlettered prophet; he who believes in Allah and in His words. Therefore follow him so that perhaps you may be rightly guided. (The Quran, chapter *The Heights,* 7:157-158)

In sum, from the above verses, the mission of the new expanded law is to liberate the humans from their burdens and yokes put on them by former restrictions that were imposed by the earlier law. The expanded knowledge frees them from their self-imposed, or rather, imposed limitations and restrictions; and their horizons are broadened further more. This is the reason why some restrictions imposed at the time of Adam were lifted at the time of Noah. Some restrictions imposed at the time of Noah were lifted at the time of Abraham. Some restrictions imposed at the time of Abraham were lifted at the time of Moses. And some restrictions imposed at the time of Moses were lifted at the time of Jesus. As Jesus himself stated in Chapter *The Family of 'Imran*:

> And I testify to that which went before me from the Torah and that I may make lawful for you some of that which has been made unlawful for you, and I have come to you with a sign from your Lord so revere Allah and obey me. (The Quran, 3:50)

This is a statement of expansion and simplification of the law of Moses by Jesus. And the law of Jesus, as well, were expanded and simplified with the prophecy of Muhammad, peace be upon him.

We witness here that the human being has been gradually liberated and freed from many restrictions and limitations as the universe expanded farther and farther and became lighter and lighter. However, this does not mean that the recordings of earlier testimonies should be subjected to destruction and oblivion. On the contrary, they need to be preserved as records of the different stages of the growth and expansion of our universe, as well as the human horizons. So that when we read the books of Adam, peace be upon him, it tells us what were the limits of our universe and of humans at that time. It is a history of faith, knowledge and human progress. So as well when we come to the book of Noah, it records for us the state of our universe at that time and the information about human knowledge, the human mind and the progress made by human beings till then. The same thing is true about the book of Abraham, peace be upon him, which is a genuine and authentic record of the progress made from the beginning of the human history until then. It is a record of both natural history as well as history of science, sociology and economy. In this respect, it is a very important record and needs to be preserved. Likewise, the book of Moses, peace be upon him, the Torah is an honest record of the progress made in our universe from all levels cosmically, naturally, scientifically, spiritually, economically and socially. It is a witness and testimony. In this respect, it has full right to be preserved, maintained and studied as an authentic source of our history. That is why the Almighty advises the Prophet, peace be upon him, in chapter *Jonah*:

> But if you are in doubt about that which we have revealed unto you, then ask those who used to read the book before you. Lo! Indeed the truth has come unto you from your Lord therefore be not of those who doubt. (The Quran, 10:94)

God is telling him to make reference to earlier records as a means of corroborating what has been newly revealed to him. In other words, the new revelation is an expansion on all the former, meaning it contains all of them in a much-expanded, simpler and lighter form.

Thus, as our universe expands further and further and its limits are stretched, the layers between the here and the hereafter become thinner and thinner, and the veils between the seen and the unseen are reduced. The distance between the Creator and the created becomes closer and closer. As the end approaches closer and closer, our universe becomes further and further enlightened because of the proximity between the universe of light and the universe of matter.

As we reach our furthermost limit that demarcates our world from the next, our feelings are mixed. We have both a feeling of rejoice and a feeling of worry and concern. We rejoice because we have reached the greatest possible expansion and the greatest possible enlightenment. But we are worried and concerned because we are reaching the end, the absolute expansion, the absolute enlightenment and the final explosion. The inner world has become the outer and the outer world has sunken inward. Those who were connected to the inner world and had an inner life, they are the outer now, the superior and above. Those who had but the outer, in the erstwhile have moved lower and sunken into the depths and abyss the void of nothingness.

> The life of this world has been made seemly unto those who disbelieve so they mock at those who believe but those who safeguard their souls will be above them on the day of resurrection and Allah gives provision to whosoever He pleases without calculation. (The Quran, chapter *The Cow*, 2:212)

The entire cosmic system will be in reversed order. Those who were up will be low, and those who were low will be raised. Those who were in the east will be brought to the west and those who were in the west will rise to the east. The sun will rise from the west and so will the moon. Likewise all those in the creation who are righteous: they will depart in the divine procession from the low to the high, from west to east.

> Allah is The Ally of those who believe. He takes them out from the darknesses to the light. But those who disbelieve; their allies are the false deities (*taghut*). They take them out from the light to the darknesses. Those are the people of the fire. They will abide therein forever. (The Quran, chapter *The Cow*, 2:257)

Those who are in the west, in the murky and the dark waters of the west, God will lifit them from darkness to light. As for those in the east above in the radians and the spotlight, they will be headed away by their patron, Iblis, as mentioned in the above verse: "...those who disbelieve, their allies are the false deities (*taghut*). They take them out from the light to the darknesses."

Behold, the values have been confounded and the social

order upset. The poor, the beggar, the wayfarer, the stranger have become the crown kings in the kingdom of God, in the new order of the Almighty. As for those crowned kings and queens in the former worldly kingdom, they have become paupers and beggars. For God dislikes those who are arrogant and loves the weak and the humble. To this state of affairs the Prophet made reference:

> Faith began as a stranger (*ghareeb*), it will end as a stranger. Glad tidings for the strangers. (*Sahih Muslim*)

The word "*ghareeb*" stems from the word *ghurb* which means the setting place, the west. *Ghareeb* refers to those that are not visible in this life, nor are they conspicuous because of fame, renown, wealth, or status. These westerners are called the family of God and they are grouped in a verse of the Quran:

> And know that whatever you acquire as gain of war, that indeed one fifth of it belongs to Allah and the messenger and the near of kin and the orphans and the needy and the wayfarer, if you indeed believe in Allah and in that which We sent down on our servant on the day of the criterion, the day when the two hosts met. And Allah has power over everything. (Chapter *The Gains of War,* 8:41)

We can easily feel the honour bestowed on those enumerated in this verse by God regrouping Himself with them and regrouping them with His messenger. That is a distinction unsurpassable by any other, for as they are strangers on this earth, they are the lords of the next. The kingdom of God is easily accessible to them and it is inaccessible to the rich. Jesus stated in the Bible:

> It is harder for a rich person to enter the kingdom of God than for a camel to go through the eye of a needle.

CHAPTER 4

Expansion and Love

Love is the communion between the cores (hearts) of two beings, which means that the process of love is not limited between human and human. It is possible that any two entities in the creation can enter a relationship of love if both their cores connect. This explains some of the seemingly difficult sayings of Prophet Muhammad, peace be upon him, such as that referring to the Mount Uhud: "This mountain loves us and we love him." A lot of ink has been spent by scholars trying to find an explanation for this, but the simple truth is that the mountain has a heart and the Prophet has a heart, and if his heart and the mountain's heart connect in fondness and tenderness, then they are in love. This can be extended to any other two entities in our universe. The earth and the heaven are in the relationship of love. A plant and a human being can be in love. An animal and a plant can be in love if their hearts express tenderness to each other.

In the Prophet's mosque, there was a peice of wood on which he used to lean upon when he delivered a speech. However, when a new platform was later built for him and the people wanted to discard that piece of wood, something happened in the mosque that testified to the depth of love and fondness that wood had for the Prophet. The entire audience in the mosque heard it weeping. It was sad to be separated from the Prophet. This among many other cases testify to the fact that love is not restricted from one human to another, that it extends and includes the entire universe. This explains the statement of Jesus, peace be upon him, that if someone has a grain of faith and commands a mountain to move, it will move.

That is to say, a faithful is someone who has love in his heart. Faith is love and there is no faith without love. So if someone has a grain of divine love in their heart and commands a mountain to move, it will move out of love for him or her. And again, the origin of all movement is love. The night moves to day out of love, as the day seeks the night out of love. Any love that does not involve movement toward the object of our love is pretentious and an empty love; it is not a real love. Surprisingly, there are people who claim to love God and yet they make no effort to move towards him. They do not respond to His call to come towards him. All of the other creations in the universe, except the human being and the *jinn* (invisible beings made of fire), bear faith and they are all moving out of love towards God, willingly and lovingly.

> Then He turned to the heaven while it was a smoke then He said to it and to the earth: both of you come willingly or by compulsion. They both said: we come willingly. (The Quran, chapter *Explained in Detail*, 41:11)

They chose to move towards God lovingly and willingly. In the same manner moves all other members of the universe move towards God except some humans and some *jinn*. This willingness to move towards God out of love is an indication that they possess a living heart, which is the same as saying they have faith in their heart. This is also equal to saying that they have love in their heart.

Our faith is in proportion to our love, and our love is in proportion to the speed of our motion towards God. For the more we love something, the quicker we seek to reach it. In the same manner, the more we love God, the more we seek to reach him. Our love of God translates itself in terms of light.

The more we embrace that love, the more we increase in light; and as the volume of light increases in our heart, the greater our expansion and the faster our motion.

True love is the love of faith. It is called the enlightened love. It is distinct from the sensual love which is based on emotion and instinct. Sensual love does not proceed from the heart proper, even though we think it does. Rather, it emanates from our senses. It is lustful and voluptuous. It is cumbersome, physical, and transient. After all, its survival depends on physical contiguity. It dies with distance. On the other hand, the enlightened love, the love of core to core, of heart to heart does not depend on physical proximity to thrive and prosper. For it transcends space and time, as anything that proceeds from the heart proper lies beyond the scope of time and space, and beyond all calculation. It is without measure or count. In this respect, we understand most clearly the idea of a man loving a mountain and a mountain loving a man. Most obviously, this love cannot be sensual. It cannot be a carnal love, for there is no sensual correspondence between a human being and a mountain. So their love must be one from community of faith, unity of love, the love of God. Their love is enlightened love, transcendental and abstract. Only this form of love is true and genuine and it redounds to a spiritual uplifting.

Normally we see that the love of near relatives is mainly one of sensuality and emotion. For this reason people fail to connect to a relative who happens to be an enlightened individual in a proper relationship of love, the love of the heart. Many great masters and teachers could not succeed in communicating their light to their own children when these children remain connected to them only emotionally. When a relationship is sentimentalized, it loses its enlightened aspect, for a sentimental love is a benighted love. It is based on the love of the flesh and the blood and it goes as far as flesh and blood can go. As passionate as it may be, it is short-lived and transitory.

Take for example the case of Abu Talib, the uncle of the Prophet, who sacrificed so much to protect shelter him against the onslaught of his opponents in Mecca. So much did he suffer for the sake of the Prophet, peace be upon him. Yet his love for the Prophet was based on sentiment and emotion (*hamiyyah and asabiyyah)*. Since he failed to love the Prophet in the true manner, the enlightened love of the heart, he never embraced the message of Islam brought to him. On the other hand, Bilal who was an Abyssinian, slave, and stranger in Mecca, succeeded in loving the Prophet in the proper way and embraced the faith that he was taught. He attained salvation where the uncle of the Prophet failed to.

This poses a challenge to many who happen to be closely related to a great teacher, for if they continue to see him with the eye of sentiment and emotions then they are barred from attracting his light. On the contrary, we see that the disciples who succeed in borrowing from his light are those who are in no way sentimentally related to him; and in this manner they are advantaged to relate to him from core to core, from heart to heart, and they have less sentimental obstacles.

If a disciple sentimentalizes his or her teacher, then the disciple is shut out from the light of the teacher's heart. For a person whose father, he or she happens to be a teacher will need to treat his father as a students would, if he or she wants to inherit his father. Otherwise, he or she will only inherit from him material possession that may leave behind. As for his father's light and knowledge, none will pass unto him.

CHAPTER 5

Expansion and Trust

We said that not only humans possess a heart, but that other entities in the creation possess a heart too. For example, mountains possess a heart, plants possess a heart, oceans possess a heart, the earth possesses a heart, and the firmament possesses a heart. In brief, a heart is the core of any particular entity. So they all possess a core and therefore they possess a heart as well.

The capacity of an entity does not come from the size of its body, nor does its force come from its hardness, nor does its speed depend on its size or height. The capacity of a particlar entity depends on the quality of its heart. Its speed, its force, its capacity, and its luminosity all depend on the expansiveness of its heart. Its ability to stretch out and open up depends in turn on its flexibility, suppleness, smoothness, resilience, and elasticity. The heart is the house of God proper where He manifests Himself and where His many beautiful qualities as well as majestic ones are deployed. In this manner, God will manifest Himself to a mountain in her heart, and will manifest Himself to earth in her heart, and will manifest Himself to the heavenly firmament in her heart, and so as well, God will manifest Himself to many humans in their hearts.

These manifestations differ in volume and size, depending on the capacity of that particular heart. Just as the Prophet, peace be upon him, said: “Hearts are vessels, some are more capacious than others.” As we remarked earlier, this capaciousness does not depend on the size of the body of the entity, but rather on the smoothness and flexibility of its heart. The more flexible it is, the more expansive it becomes. In this way, we conceive that even though God is one and He manifests Himself to all living hearts in the same manner, their conceptions vary in clarity, in measure, in number and in beauty depending of the capacity of their variousness. A heart of a greater capacity will more truly reflect a divine manifestation than another of a lesser capacity. A heart with greater expansiveness will have a truer conception of God’s manifestations than a less expansiveness one. So while they all reflect and conceive divine manifestations and share a measure of truthfulness, one can be a truer reflection than another, and one can be of a better conception than another.

> And follow the best of that which has been sent down unto you from your Lord before the punishment comes upon you suddenly while you are not aware. (The Quran, chapter *The Flocks*, 39:55)

The “best” here refers to the best conception of a word of God, of His names, and the best reflection of His manifestations. God has not denied the term good to be attributed to the lesser conceptions, or the lesser reflections. Rather, He absorbs us to follow the best, for the best is the closest to Him, is the quickest venue to Him, and is the shortest route to Him.

> They (who are in the heavens and in the earth) are those who call (their Lord) and seek the mean to their Lord whichever is closest, and they hope for His Mercy and they fear His punishment. Verily the punishment of your Lord is something to wary off. (The Quran, chapter *The Night Journey*, 17:57)

Here the word “closest” is synonymous to the word best. To follow the best from God means to take the closest access to Him.

We said earlier that the best given to us is the best reflection and conception of the word of God, which is also the newest release from God. That newest release from God is known as *dhikr muhdath* (renewed remembrance).

> Nothing comes to them of renewed remembrance from their Lord but they listen to it while they are sporting. (The Quran, chapter *The Prophets,* 21:2)

> And no renewed remembrance comes to them from Al-Rahman, but that they turn their faces away from it in arrogance. (The Quran, chapter *The Poets*, 26:5)

The words in these verses "renewed remembrance" mean this is the best and the most conclusive message of God compared to the earlier ones, which are lesser fragments of truth, and not the whole truth. Only the newest represents the whole truth as newly revealed by God. This renewal of the message of God goes hand in hand with the periodic renewed expansion of the universe. With every new expansion of our universe, there is a new expansion from the word of God and with that goes a new conception of the word of God. Only the actual and current conception of the word of God can be considered as the actual word of God, and the former conception can be considered only as traces of the present conception.

God's kingdom has only increase and progress, and a decrease and regress cannot be suffered therein. That will amount to walking in the reverse direction to the way of God. This is why God wants us, with all justification, to follow the best, the newest, and the closest; if not then you will suffer from darkness and annihilation. To stay living and enlightened, one must keep up-to-date with the divine manifestations and the newly released message regarding the most recent events in the Kingdom of God, as well as the entire universe and to keep abreast with the new advancements of the divine process. Whoever falls back, falls into darkness and whoever lags behind, lags in the quagmire of nothingness. To avoid that, one is required to keep himself up-to-date and embrace the newest message released from God. Only by virtue of that newest message can anyone be able to repel darkness and evil as we read in the Quran:

> And the good and the evil are not equal. Push back (evil) with that which is most excellent. Behold! The one between whom and you there there was emnity, it is as though he will become an ally and intimate friend. (Chapter *Explained in Detail*, 41:34)

CHAPTER 6

The Human Heart

We said that not only humans possess a heart, but that mountains, plants, earth and heaven all possess one as well. In fact that's what we learn from the story in which God offered the trust (*amanah*) to the heavens, the earth, and the mountains and asked them to bear and to carry it. They offered their apologies and asked the Almighty to excuse them. They said *we are scared and weak and cannot bear it.* The offer was finally made to the human being, the last one to come on the stage of life, and he accepted the offer of such responsibility that could not be bourn by such mighty creations of God as the heavens, the mountains and the earth.

How could a tiny creature like the human accept to bear the offer? If those mighty creations are not equal to the task, how could a human be? God informs us that when the human being accepted the offer, he was completely ignorant and had no knowledge about measure and balance, and no responsibility can be carried out without these two fundamenta[illegible]ools. The first tool is the book which contains knowledge a
and the other is wisdom which is represented by b
and measurement. So how could the human be
possession of these two tools, offer to take char

The answer to this question lies in t

ply trusted God. What does trust in God mean? It
pend and rely in the mercy of God. So, even though
being was the most ignorant among them, the least
/ notion of justice or balance, the one thing he had in his heart was the faith in the Magnanimity of God. He had trust in the Mercy and Benevolence and Clemency of the Almighty, and because he trusted God, he won the biggest prize: the trust of God (*amanah*). He trusted God and God trusted him.

God entrusted him with the most sacred, most hidden, most worthy of His Names. He relied on God and God relied on him. Further, He relied on him to be the bearer of His spirit. He loved God and God loved him, but the foundation of love is trust. There is no love without trust, and there is no trust without love. He has become the Trustee of God, the beloved of the Almighty. They trust God, and God trusts them. This is what faith means. To have faith in someone is to trust them, and to trust him is to love him. And those who have faith love God most, as mentioned in the Quran:

> And among mankind is such who takes equals to Allah; they love them as much as they love Allah but those who believe are those that love Allah the most and if only those who wrong their own souls could see, when they will see the punishment, that the power altogether is for Allah and that verily Allah is formidable in punishment. (Chapter *The Cow*, 2:165)

> O you who believe! Whoever recants his religion from among you, then in time Allah will bring a people whom He loves and who love Him; they are gentle towards the believers and they are firm towards the disbelievers; they strive in the way of Allah and they do not fear the blame of any blamer. That is the favour of Allah, He gives to whom He pleases and Allah is all encompassing all knowing. (Chapter *The Heavenly Food Bowl*, 5:54)

CHAPTER 7

Trust and Love

The human being, regardless of his ignorance, lack of balance, and equilibrium, had put his trust in God and took upon himself the task of carrying the offer of God. That offer was none other than the trust (*amanah*).

> We indeed presented the trust to the heavens and the earth and the mountain but they refused to undertake it and they were concerned thereof. But the human being undertook it. Verily he indeed was without wisdom without knowledge. So that Allah may punish the hypocritical men and women, and those men and women who ascribe partners to Allah and so that Allah may turn to the believing men and women and Allah is indeed Oft-Forgiving Most Merciful. (The Quran, chapter *The Confederates*, 33:72-73)

The heavens, the earth and the mountains refused to trust God and that refusal was based on their knowledge, enlightenment, and balance. That is to say, they based their decision on what they knew, but beyond all knowledge nothing lies but trust. Where knowledge ends, trust begins. Where knowledge stops, love begins. Where science pulls over, faith starts off. This was the mistake made by these colossal creations of God. They judged God based on their knowledge. They knew not that a slave is not supposed to deal with his master on the basis of knowledge, but rather on the basis of trust. For the knowledge of a created being can never encompass the reality of the Creator. The Creator will always lie out of the scope of the creation's knowledge. That space, that void, that vacuum which lies between the Creator and the created can only be bridged by trust and love and faith. Not by knowledge, signs, calculations, or mathematical formulas.

> So when their messenger came to them with clear signs, they exulted in that which they had from the knowledge and befell them that which they used to mock at. (The Quran, chapter *The Forgiver*, 40:83)

In this verse, God refers to the people who, instead of trusting God and trusting their messengers, put their trust in their knowledge. That is a fatal mistake made by so many who seek to know God. What they think is trusting God is rather trusting their knowledge. To trust God, one will have to first admit total ignorance, total weakness, and total inadequacy. Once one has made that confession, then can he enter into the relationship of trust, love and faith with God.

> The day Allah will gather the messengers and then He will say, 'What were you given as a response?' They will say, 'There is no knowledge for us. Verily indeed You are The Knower of the things hidden.' (The Quran, chapter *The Heavenly Food Bowl*, 5:109)

So if the messengers admit their ignorance, who else can know better? Who else is wiser than them? Perhaps the most eloquent statement regarding limits of knowledge of the slaves and the trust in the knowledge of God is the statement of Jesus, peace be upon him:

> And when Allah said 'O Jesus son of Mary! Is it you that said to the people: take me and my mother as two deities

> other than Allah' He said 'Glory be unto You It is not for me to say anything that is not right for me. If I did say it then You surely know it. You surely know all that is within myself but I do not know what is within Yourself. Verily you only are The Knower of the things hidden. (The Quran, chapter *The Heavenly Food Bowl*, 5:116)

This statement best describes the limit of the human knowledge. The furthest he knows is what is in his heart, but what is in God's heart, no one knows, and because no one knows what is in God's heart, the ultimate recourse for a human being is to surrender his knowledge, confess his ignorance, and trust the knowledge of God. This is what constitutes the basis of faith. This is what the human being chose to take as a way, the way of God. The way of faith, trust, and love is obviously the best and the nearest access to God. While the heavens, the earth, and the mountains based their decisions on their knowledge which is to say that they put their trust in what was in their hearts, the human being on the contrary put his trust in knowledge of God, in what is in God's heart. He trusted God's Mercy and knew that nothing else could be in the heart of the Almighty, but what is good. Which means that only grace, forgiveness, mercy, clemency can proceed from Him. So he put his trust in the clemency of God, and God returned his trust for trust. God trusted him with his hidden name, which is a key that opens the doors of all the treasuries of God.

The treasures of His mercy in count is a hundred mercy. In reality, it is infinity. By trusting in the mercy of God, the human being knew that he could not go wrong. For he recognized that God had written mercy upon Himself, as it states in the Quran:

> Say: for whom is all that is in the heavens and in the earth? Say: for Allah. He has written the mercy upon Himself. Surely He will gather you to the day of resurrection; there is no doubt in it. Those who have caused

> loss to their own souls, it is those who do not believe. (Chapter *The Cattle*, 6:12)

This means that God has written upon Himself that He is the Lord of mercy, and that those who believe in Him and put their trust and faith in His mercy, will be only shown mercy. He will inscribe faith in their hearts and the hidden name of his mercy, which is only revealed to lovers. From the Quran, we read about His hidden name:

> You will not find a people, who believe in Allah and the last day, loving with fondness those who defy Allah and His messenger, even though they may be their fathers or their children or their brethren or their clan. These are the ones He has written faith in their hearts and has strengthened them with a spirit from Him. And He will make them enter into gardens beneath, which rivers flow to abide therein forever. Allah is pleased with them and they are pleased with Him and these are the party of Allah and verily the party of Allah, they are the prosperous. (The Quran, chapter *The Arguing Woman*, 58:22)

Those are the faithful men and women in whose hearts God has written faith, which means His love and His hidden name of mercy. In addition to writing faith on their hearts, He supported that written word with a spirit from Him. That Spirit is known as the Holy Spirit called *Ruhul Quds*.

The Holy Spirit serves as a reinforcement and a source of support and reassurance for what is written in the hearts of the faithful. When they witness the presence of the Holy Spirit, they feel reassured that what is written in their hearts is indeed the certain Truth from God. In this respect, the Holy Spirit is a means of verification and authentication for the individual spirits that are embedded in the hearts of the various believers. However, only one individual carries the Holy Spirit in his heart while the rest of the believers carry the traces and marks of it.

This individual who carries the Holy Spirit in his heart is the principle trustee of God and his trust from God is the Holy Spirit.

CHAPTER 8

The Trustee and the Trust

We have seen indicated in the foregoing verses that God has written His name of mercy in the hearts of individual believers. That word of mercy is the name of the Holy Spirit, which is entrusted only to the principal trustee of God. That principal trustee is at different times either a Prophet or a representative of a Prophet. The Holy Spirit is the universal spirit by which the entire universe is kept alive. It is the universal soul to which individual souls relate. The name of this Holy Spirit is written on the tablet of the heart of individual believers, so that when the Holy Spirit comes to them, it serves as a means of consolidation and verification.

> Say it was brought down in truth by the spirit of holiness from your Lord so as to reinforce those who believe and as a guidance and glad tidings to those who have submitted. (The Quran, chapter *The Bee*, 16:102)

In this verse we are told in this verse that the Holy Spirit strengthens those who believe, guides them and brings them glad tidings. That glad tidings regards the mercy and the grace of God.

The Prophet said to Hassan bin Thabit, the poet of Madinah, who used to defend the Muslims against the poets of Mecca:

"Attack them with your poetry and the Holy Spirit is with you." That is to say, the Holy Spirit will support you and strengthen you. Another reference to the Holy Spirit in the Quran is in relationship to Jesus, peace be upon him:

> Those messengers, We favoured some of them above others. Among them were such Allah spoke to and some of them He raised in ranks and We granted unto Jesus son of Mary the clear signs and We strengthen him with the spirit of the holiness. And had Allah so pleased then those who came after them would not have fought with one another after that all the clear signs had come unto them but they disagreed and among them are those who believed and yet among them are others who disbelieved. And had Allah so pleased they would not have fought with one another but Allah does what He wills. (The Quran, chapter *The Cow*, 2:253)

These verses outlines that the role and the function of this universal spirit, which God sends time to time to a chosen slave of His on earth as a means of support and reassurance to the believers.

Although the believers can read the name of God that is written in their hearts, they still need a way to verify and authenticate what they read in order to ascertain it in their hearts. The Holy Spirit thus serves as a means of authentification, and it is borne only by the Trustee. He carries the essence of the spirit and the others carry only the name and the reflections of the reality of the spirit.

It is this Holy Spirit that was presented as a trust to the heavens, the earth and the mountains. They refused to take it and were afraid to do so, but the human being, out of trust in God, accepted the trust of God. He trusted God and God trusted him, and chose him as a trustee to bear His trust, to carry His Holy Spirit. The human carried off the biggest prize in the kingdom of God, for there is nothing in the kingdom of God equal in worth and merit to His Holy Spirit. When it was offered to the human being, he was in possession of neither knowledge nor justice. He had no idea of either balance or measurement. However, the one thing he was in possession of was trust in God. Trust in His mercy, faith and love. And by this, he won the prize. Not because of his knowledge, but because of his trust. The heavens, the mountains, and the earth refused to accept the trust because they calculated the consequences based on their knowledge; and this is a mistake. In dealing with God, we do not rely on our knowledge; we only rely on the knowledge of God. That reliance on the knowledge of God is what is called trust in God.

It was fortunate for the human being that he was so ignorant, innocent, naïve, uncalculatingly, unmathematical, weak, and meek. And with that weakness, he won the biggest prize. Because he looked at his weakness and knew that he cannot compete with the rest based on strengths and muscles, he chose the best solution: to leave his affairs in the hands of God. In which case, he chose to act with the power of God and not his own, and with the knowledge of God, not his own. He was content with the knowledge of God and this earned him peace and tranquility. As Jesus, peace be upon him, said: "you know what is in my heart, I do not know what is in Yours," for no one knows what is in God's heart. By confessing our ignorance, we are given knowledge. The knowledge of the created will never encompass the knowledge of the Creator. What you do not know is always more than what you know and you will never finish learning.

CHAPTER 9

Adam, Between Faith and Knowledge

God teaches us that when Adam, peace be upon him, took the trust, which is the Holy Spirit, his choice to carry it was not based on knowledge, calculation, or judgment, for he was in possession of none of these. Since he possessed none of these tools of analysis and assessment, he was in no position to measure and calculate the consequences of his decision. This state of affairs left him no other course of action but to fall back on trust, even though he did not know the consequences of his decision. However, one concept he was aware of was God's Mercy, and in that he put his trust and God returned his trust for Trust. God therefore, put His trust in Adam, peace be upon him. That trust was the Holy Spirit.

> We indeed presented the trust to the heavens and the earth and the mountains but they refused to undertake it and they were concerned thereof but the human being undertook it. Verily he indeed was without wisdom, without knowledge. (The Quran, chapter *The Confederates*, 33:72)

This verse is telling us that Adam, peace be upon him, was only a man at the moment when he undertook to carry the trust. The reality of that manhood in essence is ignorance and lack of judgment. This is the state of affairs of a human being before he receives the spirit. A human being minus the spirit is no other than a house of ignorance, benightment, and lack of judgment. On the other hand, knowledge, judgment and guidance only came to him with the reception of the spirit from God. The state of Adam before he received the spirit was "without wisdom, without knowledge." After he received the spirit, his state and status changed from lack of knowledge and wisdom, to having wisdom and knowledge. These qualities of enlightenment are not essentially characteristic of a human being. Instead, they are endowed to him by virtue of the spirit he carries. This is so important for a human to understand: he, in his origins, was without any knowledge, without any light, without any judgment, but that they were conferred upon him by the Spirit for God and as he was at the beginning definitely he will be at the end.

That is to say that as he was without knowledge and judgment at the beginning, he will be without them at the end. Those faculties of understanding and perception were only lent to him and they will be claimed back from him. So, as in the beginning, before he received the spirit without knowledge and perception, he again becomes that same person at the end.

> The day We will roll up the heaven like the way a scroll is rolled over the books. As We started its creation the first time We will repeat it (a second time) that is a promise on Us and We surely are going to put it into effect. (The Quran, chapter *The Prophets*, 21:104)

As it was in the beginning, our state was one of ignorance and lack of judgment, so shall it be for us at the end. We were born without it and we will die without it. God says:

> Allah has raised you out of the wombs of your mother when you knew nothing and He made for you the hearing and the (degrees of) sights and the hearts so that perhaps you may offer gratitude. (The Quran, chapter *The Bee*, 16:78)

Hence, we were born without it and we will die without it. The beginning and end are always the same.

We are only given knowledge, understanding, hearing, and sight as tools to help ourselves accomplish the journey from the beginning to the end. That beginning was God and that end is God; we started off from Him and we will return back to Him. Knowledge is only a means not an end; it is a means by which we can trace our path back to where we came from. From God we came and back to God we go; from the dust we came and back to dust we go. Between the beginning and the ending is what constitutes the journey; what do we need the means for if we have the end? What do we need knowledge for if we have God to hold on to the means? When we have the end in our hand, it is purposeless and meaningless. What do we need a ride for when we have arrived home? The journey is over. The peregrinations are over. The pilgrimage is over. The pilgrim has finally arrived at the sanctuary and has thrown away one's stick.

> Do you remember the encounter between Moses and the Almighty? When the Almighty asked him, 'O! Moses, what is that in your right hand?' Moses said, 'It is my rod; on it I lean, with it I beat down fodder for my flocks, and in it I find other uses.' God said to him, 'Throw it Moses.' He threw it and behold! It was a snake active in motion. Allah said, 'Seize it and fear not, we shall return it at once to its former condition.' (The Quran, chapter *Ta-Ha*, 20:17-21)

The significance of God asking Moses to throw away his staff is to let him know that his journeys were over; that his toils were over; that his wanderings were over. He has finally reached his final destination. What does he need a staff for anymore? If he was to lean on it as a means of support, he has indeed found a real support: God Himself who has now strengthened him with

His Holy Spirit. If it was a means of providing for his flocks, the best provision for his flock, which symbolically means his people, has come to him. That provision is not fodder, nor is it the produce of any plant, but the provision of God, which is *manna* and *salwa*, honey and flour showered with peace and tranquility. After his thirst and hunger and long struggle and labor to earn his livelihood, the doors of the heavenly granaries were widely opened to him. No more wanderings and no more labors. Moses was home now with God. He threw his stick away and betook himself to the pleasures of home and took off his shoes and entered the Holy Sanctuary: the abode of the Holy Spirit. At the same time, when Moses reached home, God says to Moses:

> Verily I am your Lord therefore take off your shoes for indeed you are in the sanctimonious valley of Tuwa. (The Quran, chapter *Ta-Ha*, 20:12)

At this point Moses took off his shoes, entered the Holy Sanctuary, and he is invested with the Holy Spirit. Does he need his staff anymore? Does he need his shoes anymore? Does he need to wander around anymore? He reached the end: all means are now useless. This is the picture of the end of Moses's journey that began from the day he departed from home, from God, and his final homecoming. Moses arrived home, the shepherd returned, but the flock was still abroad left to the mercy of the beasts of prey: pharaoh and his powers. God sent Moses off to go and bring his flock home, give the message, and warn those beasts who prey on the innocent flocks. This constitutes the mission of Moses. Moses already found the way to get home to God and so is qualified to go and guide the rest home. That was the only mission for Moses.

Moses, peace be upon him, on the day in which he encountered God in the mountain of Tur, was like Adam, peace be upon him, on the day in which God blew the spirit into him. Both events took place in the same valley. As God said to Adam:

> And We said 'O Adam! Dwell you and your wife in tranquility in the garden and eat freely thereof wherever you two wish but do not come close to this tree, lest you two become of those who do wrong to their own souls. (The Quran, chapter *The Cow*, 2:35)

While God said to Moses and his people:

> We said, 'Go down there from all of you together,' and if ever there comes unto you from Me a guidance, so whoever follows My guidance, then there will be no fear on them nor will they grieve. (The Quran, chapter *The Cow*, 2:38)

God made the same promise to Adam and Eve as he did to Moses and his people. The promise was, "Come home, My Home, into My Garden, into Jerusalem." This welcoming home was not unqualified, God put a caution along with the glad tidings, "Do not approach this tree lest you bring harm on yourself." This was the caution pronounced to Adam and Eve as to Moses and his companions, "enter the gate prostrating and ask for forgiveness."

However, Adam and Eve transgressed against the word of God:

> But the satan caused them to slip there from the garden so he caused them to exit from that which they were in before (tranquility and peace). Then We said 'Come down. Some of you being enemy of the others and there will be for you in the earth a station and a temporary enjoyment for a little while.' (The Quran, chapter *The Cow*, 2:36)

Like unto Adam and his companion, the people of Moses, also transgressed against the word of God:

> But those who wronged their own souls changed the

> word which was told to them for another word so We sent down upon those who had wronged their own souls a plague from the heaven for that they used to renegade. (The Quran, chapter *The Cow*, 2:59)

Adam had lost his garden where he lived in euphoria and felicity and the people of Moses lost their garden as well, where they lived in euphoria and felicity.

CHAPTER 10

The Holy Spirit and Knowledge

Some of the contenders of the Prophet Muhammad, peace be upon him, asked him about the Spirit and he replied:

> They ask you about the spirit, say this spirit is from the commandment of your Lord and from the knowledge you are given only a little. (The Quran, chapter *The Night Journey*, 17:85)

Now the statement, "and from the knowledge you are given only a little" refers to those who brought the question about the nature of the spirit, and God tells them that since they are not under the influence of the Holy Spirit their knowledge is of but very little. Even the little that they know may not even be called knowledge. This amounts to saying that knowledge comes to us with the receiving of the spirit, and that without it we are devoid of any understanding, as we read:

> He who has made everything that He has created in excellence and He began the creation of the human being from clay. Then He made his descent from the essence of a liquid which is very delicate. Then He made him even and breathed His Spirit into him and He made for you the hearing the sight and the understanding. Little is the thanks that you offer. (The Quran, chapter *The Prostration*, 32:7-9)

If you give little thanks, only a little knowledge is given to you. If you give more thanks, more knowledge will be given to you. An increase in thanks qualifies us for a greater breathing of the spirit into us. With the greater breathing of the spirit into us a greater knowledge comes to us. For with each new breath of the Spirit we are given new hearing, new sight and new heart. With every new hearing, new sight and new heart a new knowledge is born. As long as we increase in gratitude to God we correspondingly increase in our sensibilities and consciousness. That means the capacity of our sight and our heart increases. We will never stop increasing in knowledge as long as we increase in thanks to God. As God mentions on the tongue of Moses:

> And when your Lord proclaimed 'if you offer gratitude I will give you increase but if you be ungrateful surely my punishment is mighty. (The Quran, Chapter *Abraham*, 14:7)

In a lighter manner, God exalted the Prophet to saying this prayer:

> [...] Oh my Lord, increase me in knowledge. (The Quran, Chapter *Ta-Ha*, 20:114)

To say, "God increase me in knowledge," is as good as saying, "God increase me in gratitude;" and to say "God increase me in gratitude" is as good as saying "God breath in me a new spirit." When a new spirit is breathed into us we are given a new hearing, a new sight, and a new heart, which in turn bring us a new knowledge. As long as the gratitude is steady, the increase in knowledge will be steady, and if the gratitude comes to a halt then we stop increasing. At the point where our increase stops our decrease begins, and the decrease signifies decay and downfall.

Iblis was well aware of this fact and that is why he declared to

God saying:

> He said now that you have caused me to err, I will surely lay in wait for them on your path the most upright. Then, I will surely come upon them from before them and from behind them and from their right and from their left and you will not find most of them grateful. (The Quran, Chapter *The Heights*, 7:16-17)

The assault launched by Iblis on the children of Adam is to render them ungrateful, for by doing that he prevents them from increasing in knowledge. As they increase in knowledge so they increase in closeness to God and become stronger in their ways. This means that as long as they offer gratitude, they will get increase in their faculties in hearing, seeing, and understanding which in turn leads to an overall increase in their knowledge. Thus the plan of Iblis to condemn them to death is defeated by their constant offer of gratitude.

PART II

HAJJ: A HOMEWARD, HOMECOMING JOURNEY

CHAPTER 11

Hajj: An Introduction

Hajj constitutes the final phase of a long process. It is the final stage of a long journey. For this reason many wonder why Hajj proper is performed in a few days within one single month called *Dhul Hijjah*. However, the Quran refers to the "months of Hajj" indicating that Hajj does not take place within one month but rather within months.

The explanation for this is that the preparatory stages that lead up to Hajj proper are also considered Hajj. Another example of this is the saying of the Prophet, peace and blessings be upon him, "one of you is considered to be in prayer as long as he waits for prayer." This waiting period, which is considered to be the preparatory period, is considered part of the worship. Therefore if we take into consideration all the months in which preparations for Hajj take place as part of Hajj, then Hajj is months long and not a month.

This preparatory period may extend over roughly four months beginning with the month of *Ramadan, Shawwal, Dhul Q'adah* and finally the month of Hajj proper called *Dhul Hijjah*. These are three months and ten days and is approximately 100 days if we count up to the tenth day of the month of Hajj, on which the last rite of Hajj—the sacrifice—takes place. But if we count the whole month of *Dhul Hijjah* then it amounts to four months, which is about 120 days.

It takes the same number of days (120) or months (4) for a fetus to develop from liquid state (40 days) to blood state (40 days) to flesh state (40 days). At the end of this period, God sends an angel to blow in the spirit (*rooh*), the living breath, into the foetus. In a like manner, the pilgrim (*Haji*) also goes through the stages of formation like the foetus, but internally. Once the inner form is round and full in due proportions, then God breathes His spirit into him, and this is the meaning of the prophetic saying that:

> If anyone performs Hajj and has not professed obscenities or committed infidelity or incurred hooliganism he/she would come forth like the day he was first born by his mother.

This means that a well-performed Hajj is equivalent to a new birth (rebirth) free from any guilt or sin.

If, however, we start counting the beginning of the process from the month of *Sha'ban* up to the tenth day of *Dhul Hijjah*, that will amount to four months and ten days. This is equivalent to the waiting period for a widow after the demise of her spouse before she could enter in relation with another man. It takes the deceased husband four months and ten days to complete the reverse process from flesh to blood, from blood to liquid and back to the essence at which point the tie is severed completely between the dead spouse and the living, surviving wife.

> And those who are taken by death among you and they leave wives, they (the wives) should wait four months and ten (days before making any decision) about themselves. But when they reach their term, then there is no blame on you regarding that which they do concerning themselves in a fairly manner and Allah is all acquainted about all that you do. (The Quran, chapter *The Cow*, 2:234)

CHAPTER 12

Stations on the Way

The stations on the way of Hajj are five, the fifth station consisting of the actual rites of Hajj and the preceding four representing four preparatory stations that lead up to the final station of Hajj.

FIRST STATION: THE INTENTION

The first of these five stations is the that of making up one's mind, called intention. This intention is committing oneself to undertaking the assignment of pilgrimage. In other words, it means taking a vow or making a covenant with God to return to Him and to go home. The Home is God's Kingdom, paradise (*jannah),* and the patron of the Home is the Almighty Allah. So the return home to God is called *tawbah*. The declaration of that intention is the statement "*la ilaha illallah*"—Allah is the sole deity—"*Muhammad rasulullah*"—Muhammad is His messenger. This declaration means recognizing that there is no recourse but God, and that Muhammad's way to God is the way. This is the intention to migrate towards God and His Messenger. To do this, the pilgrim must take upon himself to leave everything behind—family, land, spouse (except the ones who are willing to be companions of the way), children, horses, wealth (gold and silver), and cattle, which are the seven bonds (fetters) that tie down the pilgrim to his spot. Once he makes up his mind to leave all these behind and never look back, he must therefore turn his face to his destination—namely where he is immigrating to: God, the Home and His messenger. Once he decides to choose God and the last home, then he is renouncing seven objects of the love of lust in exchange for the seven objects of the love of faith (*iman*). This renunciation is called *zuhd* and means to renounce the lesser for the better and the temporal for the lasting:

> [...] and Allah is best and lasting. (The Quran, chapter *Ta-Ha*, 20:73)

> But the hereafter is better and more lasting. (The Quran, chapter *The Most Hight,* 87:17)

Islam does not recognize anything like absolute renunciation. It is to renounce the lesser for the better and not the reverse. It is to replace every form of love of lust for love of faith, and that entails replacing the following seven: 1. Spouses 2. Children; 3. Gold; 4. Silver; 5. Horses; 6. Cattle; 7. Land.

> Love of the lusts has been made seemly unto mankind from the women and the children and the amassed treasures of gold and silver and the horses of high breed and the cattle and the farm. That is the temporary pleasure of the life of this world. But Allah, indeed with Him is the excellent place of return. (The Quran, chapter *The Family of Imran*, 3:14)

The word migration (*hijrah*) requires leaving all these behind in the quest for God and His Messenger. This was exactly what the companions of the Prophet, peace be upon him, did when they left Mecca for Medina. They left everything behind and migrated to God and His Messenger. For the statement, "*la ilaha illallah*" is a declaration of faith meaning that "I love God more than everything and thereafter I love His Messenger more than everything else." Once the pilgrim affirms the declaration of faith and breaks his ties with the seven fetters of his worldly desires, he has successfully fulfilled the requirement of the first station, which is the point of departure. If, in the course of his journey he breaks this covenant, he must therefore return back to this first station and restart. The Prophet, peace be upon him says, "Renew your faith by declaring '*la ilaha illallah*.'"

SECOND STATION: DETERMINING DIRECTION

Once the pilgrim has broken loose from the seven chains that were holding him captive and now stands free from all fetters, the second task lies in determining the direction of his journey. He must know where to turn his face. That direction is known as the *qiblah*. The practice of setting one's face towards the *qiblah* is known as *tawajjuh* and the discipline that deals with helping the pilgrim to find his bearing is called *salah*. The word *salah* means to turn your face to someone or to something which shows you are pleased with that person or thing; to turn your face away means displeasure, and to turn your face towards means pleasure and satisfaction. In this case the pilgrim has turned his face away from the seven lusts and consequently broken the seven fetters, and in reverse he has turned his face towards God, His messenger, and the home of everlastingness; showing his displeasure and dissatisfaction with the former and his pleasure and satisfaction with the latter.

It must therefore be understood when the Quran says, "God and His angels perform Salah on you" (chapter *The Cow*, 2:157), that this does not mean prayer in the form of genuflexion (*ruku'*) and prostration (*sujud*). Rather, it means that God has turned His face and looked at you with pleasure and satisfaction and so have His angels. So *salah* and *ridwaan* are equations. God's displeasure and anger is signified by His turning His f
away from a person. This is the worst of His p
who know God—the gnostics—their fear is nc
but God's turning His face away. They say th
lowed the perishable world (*dunya)* to be, He l

look upon it. And when one of the Prophet's companions was caught guilty of an offence, the Prophet, peace be upon him said:

> Leave him, indeed God must have looked at the participants of the Battle of Badr and said to them: 'Do as you please, I have forgiven you all.'

God's word and God's pleasure do not change. If He speaks, decrees, or commands, His word never changes. It must go through. If He says you are forgiven it is His word, it will never change. So is His pleasure, for if He looks at you once He will never be displeased with you ever after. His face and His word never alter and the impact of His word and His face never alter either. By His word things are allowed to be, and by His face things that came to be are given the mark of pleasure. Everything that is, has come to be by God's permission—by His word. This doesn't necessarily mean everything that exists by the pleasure of God. Permission and pleasure are two different categories of reality. By His word things come to be and by His pleasure they continue to be in pleasure. They enjoy being and they continue to be in wellness and soundness, safeguarded from change and alienation. This endurance is known as blessing (*barakah*), as distinct from His Mercy. By His word of Mercy things come to be, but they continue to be in blessing by the pleasure of His face. By the pleasure of His face it becomes written. By writing, the word becomes fixed and is given permanence. If it is not written it is subject to change.

> And prescribe for us in this world an excellent reward as well as the hereafter. Verily we have responded to you. He said: My punishment, I inflict with it whom I please and My mercy encompasses everything. However I will write it only for those who revere Me and for those who give out the sanctifying dues and for those who believe in Our signs. (The Quran, chapter *The Heights*, 7:156)

Allah effaces what He pleases and confirms (what He pleases) and with Him is the mother of the book. (The Quran, chapter *The Thunder*, 13:39)

> You will not find a people who believe in Allah and the last day loving with fondness those who defy Allah and His messenger even though they may be their fathers or their children or their brethren or their clan. These are the ones He has written faith in their hearts and has strengthened them with a spirit from Him. And He will make them enter into gardens beneath which rivers flow to abide therein forever. Allah is pleased with them and they are pleased with Him and these are the party of Allah and verily the party of Allah, they are the prosperous. (The Quran, chapter *The Arguing Woman*, 58:22)

By His word things emerged out of the ocean of mercy, but by His face such things are written, fixed and retained from submerging again into the ocean of annihilation.

> Our word of commandment for anything that We will it to happen is for Us to say to it, 'Be,' and it is. (The Quran, chapter *The Bee*, 16:40)

> She said: O my Lord! How can I have a son when no human being has ever touched me? He said: It is thus that Allah creates what He pleases. When He decrees a matter, He just says to it, 'Be,' and it is. (The Quran, chapter *The Family of Imran*, 3:47)

> It is not befitting for Allah to take a son for himself. Glory be to Him. Whenever He decrees an affair, He but says to it, 'Be,' and it is. (The Quran, chapter *Mary*, 19:35)

> The inventor of the heavens and of the earth and when He decrees a matter, He just says to it, 'Be,' and it is. (The Quran, chapter *The Cow*, 2:117)

And by His face they are given the right to be written and to continue to be and to be remembered, and what is not meant to be remembered is to be forgotten.

> Rehearse what has been inspired to you from the book and establish the prayer. Verily the prayer does refrain from the offensive and disgraceful acts and verily remembrance (*dhikr*) of Allah is the most great and Allah knows all that you fabricate. (The Quran, chapter *The Spider*, 29:45)

> Allah has promised unto the believing men and the believing women gardens beneath which the rivers flow to abide therein forever and goodly abodes in gardens of eternal felicity and the good pleasure (*ridwaan*) of Allah is the greatest (*akbar*). That is the success the most magnificent. (The Quran, chapter *The Repentance*, 9:72)

In both of the above verses the terms "*dhikr*" (remembrance) and "*ridwaan*" (pleasure of God) are qualified as "*akbar*" meaning the most great; where greatness doesn't diminish, and there is no change in status.

Therefore, if God remembers something, it comes to be, and if He looks at it, it is written and will continue to be and to be remembered. If it is not looked at, if it is not written, it will not continue to be and be remembered. This is the meaning of the Quranic verse:

> And your Lord creates what He pleases and chooses (from what He created). There is no choice for them. Glory be unto Allah and far exalted is Allah above all that they ascribe as partners to Him. (The Quran, chapter *The Stories*, 28:68)

That means the first stage of existence is to come to be and the second stage is to be chosen to continue to exist; for few are written and most are consigned to erasure and annihilation. They relapse into the ocean of nothingness. The Prophet, peace be upon him, says:

> God created the creation in darkness and then spread His light over them. Those touched by it were rightly guided. (*Sahih Bukhari*)

This means He created them all out of His mercy and chose some and raised them by His pleasure. The Face determines a choice. By His word "be" they are. Then, He looks and chooses. There is no choosing without looking. If the commandment involved both the Word and the Face, then the creature has the sanction to be and to continue to increase in being.

Therefore, the first station represents the word "*la ilaha illallah*," by this word, things are caused to be. The second station, the station of *salah*, represents God's face or God's pleasure. This is a declaration of setting one's face in the direction of God and the beginning of a quest to find His pleasure, which, once found, the face of the finder will never perish. He will be written, never to be erased. He will survive the cataclysm. His face will rise above in splendor when the ocean of nothingness will overtake everything.

> And do not invoke any other deity along with Allah. There is no deity except He. Everything will perish except His face. To Him belong the judgment and back to Him will you be returned" (The Quran, chapter *The Stories*, 28:88)

To join the divine ark known as the Throne of God (*'arsh*)and the ark of Noah is a reminder of that.

After the pilgrim has consecrated his life, meaning his

soul (*nafs*) to God, the next is to consecrate his face to God, for it is written in the books (both the Torah and the Quran), "life for life and eye for eye." When the pilgrim declared the word of faith renouncing his former life, God compensated him with a new life; and when he surrendered his face to God by turning to Him, God also turned to Him and compensated him with a new face. He lives now by God and sees by God. When this station is successfully passed, the pilgrim is ready to enter the third station. He has the password, "*la ilaha illallah,*" and he has his bearing, "*Allahu akbar.*"

THIRD STATION: PURIFICATION

The third station deals with the question of purification. After the pilgrim has been brought from death to life by the word and then given a light in his eyes by which to see his path after his blindness, the third stage is his avowal and commitment to peace. It is a commitment not to cause harm with his hands or his tongue, nor to stain his hands or his tongue with the flesh and blood of others. Rather he is to cleanse his hands and his tongue from the property, the honour and the blood of others. At this stage he must make the declaration of peace (*salam*)—to give in goodness, to take in goodness, to speak in goodness, and to be silent in goodness. However, since the hand and the tongue are grouped together in mention, it therefore indicates these two organs have something in common: the hand being most often the agent of the tongue. We eat with our hands and our tongues. Also, between the touch of the hand and the taste of the tongue there is a close affinity. When Adam, peace be upon him, ate from the tree he took the fruit with his hand and then tasted with his tongue. Therefore, the purification (*tazkiah*, or *tat'heer*) of the hands and the tongue and the two lips must go together, for it is the hands that help the tongue, and without them, the tongue has less chance of eating forbidden (*haram*).

In addition to that, the hand holds back from giving for

the sake of the mouth. Thus, the sins of the hand and the tongue both affect one common part of our being, namely: the neck and throat. The false blood that is incurred by wrongful use of the hand or wrongful exercise of the tongue, all accumulate in the neck and throat. From these rises false word which can never reach to God. This false word is called a "lie" (*kadhib*) and God does not love liars. On the hand, the true word is called *sidq*. They both depend on the type of blood. If it is the true blood then the word is a true word, and if it is the false blood then it is a false word. The pure word from the pure blood must reach up to God; the false word from the false blood will not reach beyond the supplicant's head. If you raise clean hands up to God and beg with a clean tongue your prayer will surely be answered. The charity was prescribed upon the believers to cleanse them from the sins of their hands and their tongue and to remove the false blood which was initially incurred by Adam, peace be upon him, when he ate from the tree.

The ritual of removing this false blood from the system is signified by the story of Abraham, peace be upon him, who slaughtered his child to be replaced by a ram from the heavens; or the brothers of Joseph (Yusuf), peace be upon him, who slaughtered a lamb and claimed the blood on Josseph's shirt was his blood. It was also removed from the Prophet Muhammad, peace be upon him, when he was six years old. In sum, all the prophets undergo this operation of removing the false blood except Jesus, peace be upon him.

Another reference in the Quran about the false blood is in the story of Joseph. When the bevy of ladies, upon seeing him, rose up and screamed, "*Allahu akbar*" (God is Most Great) in chorus and then cut their hands with the knife, letting the blood out.

> So when she heard about their malicious talk, she sent for them and prepared for them (couches) to recline on and gave to each of them a knife. Then she said (to Joseph): come out in front of them. So when they saw him they

> expressed in amazement at him and cut their hands and they exclaimed: God forbid. This is not a mortal being. This is but a gracious angel. (The Quran, chapter *Joseph*, 12:31)

The meaning of this episode becomes clear once we know that the prayer uttered when slaughtering a sacrifice is also "*Allahu akbar*."

It is also narrated that the Prophet, peace be upon him, had said, "Those who read the the call to prayer (the *Muazzins*), have the longest neck." The specific feature of this call to prayer is the repetition of the word "*Allahu akbar.*" This word has the effect of reducing Satan to nothing. For this reason, he keeps his distance from wherever the call to prayer (*adhan*) is called. The elongation of the necks of the *Muazzins* means that their necks are freed and liberated from the suffocating chains of sins. They have free, pure voices that reach their target. If the chains on the necks are loosened, concurrently the chains on the hands are also loosened since the hands are bound to the neck.

> And do not tie your hand to your neck (out of stinginess) and do not stretch it out completely or you will be sitting down blameworthy and weary. (The Quran, chapter *The Night Journey*, 17:29)

> We have indeed put fetters around their necks reaching up to their chins so that they are stiff necked. (The Quran, chapter *Ya-Sin*, 36:8)

> Seize him and fetter him. Then in the blazing fire burn him. The thereafter in a chain the length of which is seventy cubits, introduce him the *saqar*[to the fire that cuts into pieces]. (The Quran, chapter *The Clamour*, 69:30-32)

> When the fetters shall be in their necks and the chains, they will be dragged. (The Quran, chapter *The Forgiver*,

40:71)

With his neck and hands liberated, the pilgrim can throw with strength and hold with strength, as God said to Moses, peace be upon him, to hold the Book with strength:

> We inscribed for him in the tablets [of Torah] from everything as an admonition and a detailing of everything [and we said to him]: hold it with strength and command your people to hold unto what is the most excellent thereof. Soon I will show you the home of those who are the renegades. (The Quran, chapter *The Heights,* 7:145)

Similarly, God says John (Yahya), peace be upon him:

> O Yahya. Hold the book with all your strength and We had given him the wisdom while still a child. (The Quran, chapter *Mary*, 19:12)

God also described Abraham, Isaac (Ishaq) and Israel (Jacob), peace be upon all of them, as people of the hands and sight, meaning people of the strength:

> And remember our servants Abraham, Isaac and Jacob masters of the power and sight. (The Quran, chapter *Saad*, 38:45)

Along with the fulfillment of purification, the pilgrim is then granted with two other blessings: (1) God speaks to him (*hadith*) and (2) God looks at him (*nadhar*).

> Verily those who sell their firm pledge to Allah and their oaths for a little price, there is no share for them in the hereafter and Allah will not speak to them and will not look at them on the day of resurrection and will not sanctify them and for them there will be a painful punishment. (The Quran, chapter *The Family of Imran*, 3:77)

God says that He doesn't speak to the disbelievers. If He speaks to you, He has called you to life for His word is "be" (*kun*) and then you are. Therefore He would not speak to the disbelievers and would not look at them, because when He does, it is a sign of satisfaction and pleasure. He would not strengthen the disbelievers with the spirit of purification and peace.

> Verily those who conceal that which Allah has sent down from the book and they sell it for a trifling price, they eat nothing in their belies except the fire and Allah will not speak to them on the day of resurrection and He will not sanctify them and for them there will be a painful punishment. (The Quran, chapter *The Cow*, 2:174)

Thus purified, the pilgrim is well prepared to carry on his peregrination with a clean hand, to hold the Book strongly. At this point, his book is given to him in his right hand, the hand of strength; he is given eyes with which to see the book, a tongue to recite it, and the feet to walk the way. These four companions of the way: the eyes to see, the hands to hold, the tongue to recite and the feet to walk. The pilgrim now stands in total purity, in its two senses: purity of the soul (*tazkiyah*) and purity of the heart and body (*tahara*), both inner and outer.

> Do they not know that verily Allah, He it is who accepts the repentance from His servants and He takes the charities and that verily, Allah He it is who is The Acceptor of the repentance, the Most Merciful. (The Quran, chapter *The Repentance*, 9:104)

The pilgrim's soul is cleansed from the most deadly sin: miserliness. He has finally overcome the most difficult obstacle towards self-liberation: stinginess, the inclination of the ego to take and not to give, to hold and not to let go, to capture and not to free, and to contract and not to expand.

The hand that gives is in expansion and the one that takes is in contraction, and for every contraction there are two expansions. For this the Prophet, peace be upon him, said, "The upper hand is better than the lower." While contraction is part of the equation and it must also be exercised, one should first thoroughly learn to expand. This is because expansion is the essence in the nature of things and contraction is for the sake of regulating the expansion and disciplining it. Thus, after the pilgrim demolished this wall of selfish holding that holds his soul in confinement (as the following chapter will demonstrate), he can then experience the absolute expansion of his soul. From being an individual soul contained in one chest.

> If only he assailed the obstacle? And what do you know about what the obstacle is? It is freeing a soul in bondage, Or feeding on a day of dire hunger, To orphans who are near of kin, Or a needy one in a state most abject (The Quran, chapter *The City*, 90:11-16)

From being an individual soul contained in one chest, it now becomes a universal soul called *nafas ar-rahmaani* (the breath from the All Merciful). With this universal soul all his fetters fall off and all his iniquities are washed away. He stands in a state of absolute purity called *birr*. With reference to this *birr*, God says:

> Verily those who disbelieve and they die while disbelievers, then the fill of the earth in gold will not be accepted from any of them even though they may offer it as a ransom. Those for them there will be a painful punishment and there will be no helpers for them. You will never attain to the piety until you spend from that which you love. And whatever thing you may spend, verily Allah is all knowing about it. (The Quran, chapter *The Family of Imran*, 3:91-92)

You can observe very well the usage of the word "from" meaning part—and not all—of everything that you love. Only if you spend from what you love, you would attain *birr*. Once this universal expansion is reached, resulting in the absolute state of purity (*birr*), then the pilgrim is ready to enter into the next station: fasting.

> Have We not expanded for you your bosom? And We laid down from you your burden, Which weighed heavy on your back, And We raised for you your remembrance. (The Quran, chapter *The Expansion*, 94:1-4)

FOURTH STATION: THE PILGRIM'S OF CANDOUR

The fourth station is that of fasting with the objective of achieving *taqwa*. Fasting consists of an act of contraction in contrast to charity (*zakah*) which consists of an act of expansion. It is normal that after an expansion we would expect a contraction to follow, for two contractions cannot follow each other nor should two expansions follow each other:

> And verily with the hardship there is ease, Verily with the hardship there is ease. (The Quran, chapter *The Expansion*, 94:5-6)

Therefore, after expansion of the former station, we expect a contraction. As expansion signifies giving, contraction signifies retention and preservation of what we have taken. In the third station of *zakah*, we have given from what we love, and God in return gave us what we love—a pure universal soul.

> And by a soul and how He extended its creation, And then He inspired it to know its transgression and its self-guard, Indeed he is prospered one who has sanctified it, And indeed he lost one who has stunted it. (The Quran, chapter *The Sun*, 91:7-10)

The pure universal soul, which we have received, needs retention, good preservation, and a contractive mode of action. This mode is fasting, which earns us *taqwa*. Linguistically, *taqwa* means protection or shield—this shield is a reference to a dress of armour that is called *libaas at-taqwa*. The garment of *taqwa* is a panoply, a protective attire of white cloth, which the new pure universal soul must be dressed with. The choice of white is to warn the wearer from coming into contact, rather, not even close to, any stain that might compromise the immaculateness of the attire. There are injunctions in the Quran which have the imperative tone of "do not approach" (with regards to) adultery and fornication, meaning, don't indulge in any talk with sexual undertones called '*rafath*.' Especially in the presence of opposite sexes, utterance of such sexual innuendos mark stains on the attire of taqwa.

In a like manner, God said to Adam, peace be upon him, "do not go near this tree" because Adam and his wife Eve (Hawwa) were both attired in this immaculate garment and they were warned not to get close to any stain. That meant not even talking about it, as that would rouse their desire for it. Speaking of something is like eating it and relishing it. For this reason, God equates backbiting with eating the flesh of the other—a common cannibalism that raises no hair! God also says don't get close to the property of an orphan—that is, don't even discuss it with an exception here: only speak about it if that means helping to invest it in a useful way for the sake of the orphan.

> And do not come near to adultery. It indeed is an act of injustice and an evil way. And do not kill the soul which Allah has made sacred except in truth. Whoever is killed wrongfully, We have indeed given authority to His heir but let him (not the heir) not exceed the limits of just retribution (*qisas*) in killing. For He (the heir) most cer
> is helped (by Allah). And do not come nea
> of the orphan except by way of goodness un
> the fullness of his strength and fulfil the pron

> promise is certainly going to be answered for. (The Quran, chapter *The Night Journey,* 17:32-34)

> And when We said unto the angels: prostrate yourselves for Adam. So they prostrated themselves except Iblis. He refused and he grew arrogant and was of those who were disbelievers. (The Quran, chapter *The Cow,* 2:34)

With regards to a pious retreat (*i'tikaaf*), once the devotee makes it bound upon himself, he must not come close to anything like making sexual hints to one's own wife.

> It has been made lawful for you in the night of the fasting to approach your wives. They are a garment for you and you are a garment for them. Allah is fully aware that you used to cheat your own souls but He has accepted your repentance and has pardoned you. Therefore now hold intercourse with them and seek that which Allah has written for you and eat and drink until the white thread becomes distinct for you from the black thread of the dawn. Then complete the fast up till the night and do not hold intercourse with them while you are in retreat in the mosques. Those are the boundaries of Allah therefore do not come near them. Thus Allah makes clear His signs for the mankind perhaps they will guard their own souls. (The Quran, chapter *The Cow,* 2:187)

Know that getting near "a stain" can be through three means: by listening, by looking, or by talking. To listen to talk about something brings you close to it; to look at something brings you close to it; and to talk about something brings you close as well. May God forbid, if the stain occurs, then another charity must be handed. This charity is called *zakatul fitr*: the compensations for breaking your fast. Even though you did not break your fast by eating food, or drinking water, or through sexual intercourse; yet the foulness in speech or giving ear to foul speech, or stealing immodest glances, are all considered fast-breakers. Therefore the penalty applies, which if given, the stain fades away and the attire of *taqwa* stands again spotless. However, the danger of staining always lurks around and the risk of being torn is always a matter of concern. Imagine a gentleman or a lady dressed in a long white gown and walking through a forest with thorns on every side and branches hanging loose. If he or she ever wishes to come out with his gown intact, he would have to take every step with extreme care, by looking at where he places the next step: looking right, then looking left and then taking a step, and so on, until he can finally exit safe and sound. This is the example of a person who is dressed in his garment of *taqwa* and lives in our world; he would have to be as careful, if not more. Once someone asked Abu Huraira, a companion of the Prophet, about the meaning of *taqwa*. He replied to him, "Come, I will show you." Then he entered a field strewn with thorns and began to walk, lifting one step and checking for a clean spot before putting his foot down until he crossed the field, then he turned around and said to him, "This is *taqwa*."

With regards to fasting, the Prophet, peace be upon him said:

> If one of you is fasting he should not entertain sexual innuendos or commit acts of disobedience, nor commit acts of ignorance (argument, fight, altercations). If anyone insults him or seeks to fight with him he should say: 'I'm fasting, I am fasting' or 'I am a fasting person.'

He declares himself as one who is fasting and wearing his dress of peace, the dress of *taqwa*—for if he involves in fighting or quarrelling, his dress might get in the process stained or torn. As experience shows, when people get into a row or a fight they most often come out with their dresses either tarnished at the least or torn at the most. For this reason, the Prophet says that your fast is *junna*—a protective shield for you. It most surely will protect you if you don't take in professing obscenities, committing acts of disobedience, fighting, quarrelling or rowing. Such acts will surely make a crack through your shield and expose you to harm and injury. So remind yourself and remind the others that you are fasting, and fasting from every form of wrongdoing—that you are declaring peace with everyone.

> And the servants of the Ar-Rahman, those who walk on the earth gently and when they are addressed by the ignorant ones they say: 'Peace.' (The Quran, chapter *The Criterion*, 25:63)

When God put Adam and his partner, Eve, in the garden, He dressed them in beautiful flowing white robes and said to them, *eat of everything within the Garden but do not cross the boundaries of the garden and take fruits of that tree yonder.* That tree was only slightly beyond the boundary of their Garden. Satan envied their blissful state and the gorgeous raiment of *taqwa*, which is the best garb. He vowed to strip them of their beauty and to show them their starkness. To succeed in this scheme, Satan found no best means of tricking them then to trivialize what they had—which was the best—and to magnify in their eyes what they supposedly didn't have. He therefore convinced them to minimize what they have and to desire what only existed in imagination and to let go of their certitude for mere doubt and speculation. He instigated in them the love of what is foreign, exotic and convinced them to overlook the familiar bounties of God and exchange the peaceful quietness and tranquility of their life for excitement and sensation of adventure. This is the trick by which Satan caused Adam to trip; and he continues to cause more of his children to fall by the same trick—who are invariably the same at core. A nickel of certitude is worthier than thousands of dollars of doubt. Stick to this and Satan has no weapon against you. This is *taqwa*.

Children of Adam wake-up! Beware!

> And thus We have revealed it as an Arabic Quran and We have given in it many facets to the warning so that

> perhaps they will revere Allah or perhaps it will occasion for them a renewed remembrance. For exalted is Allah The King, The Truth and do not be in haste with the Quran before its revelation to you is consummated and say: O My Lord increase me in knowledge. And indeed We gave Our assignment to Adam beforetime but he forgot and We did not find in him a firm resolution. And when We said to angels: bow down to Adam they did bow down except Iblis—he refused (out of arrogance). So We said: O Adam this (Iblis) is an enemy for you and your spouse so beware lest he drives the two of you out of the garden and you will be in misery. It is given that in this garden you will not go hungry nor naked. (The Quran, chapter *Ta-Ha*, 20:113-118)

Adam ate from the tree and so did his wife and they became stark naked. They lost their garment of *taqwa*.

> Then He said: therein you shall live and therein you shall die and there from you shall be brought forth. O children of Adam! We indeed have sent down upon you garment which covers your nudity and as ornamentation and yet the garment of God's reverence that is the best. That is of the signs of Allah so that they may oft-remember. (The Quran, chapter *The Heights*, 7:25-26)

If the pilgrim, at this stage, stains his dress and the stain is minor, then it can be corrected by expiatory charity. If it is serious he may have to go back and start to reclimb again. If he succeeds in maintaining his *birr* and *taqwa* intact then he can move on to the final station. The connection between *birr* and *taqwa* is often emphasized in the Quran and they are mentioned together.

> Help each other to practice *birr* and *taqwa* and to keep away from their opposites—withholding (*ithm*) and transgression (*'udwan*).

> O you who believe! Do not violate the rights of Allah nor the sacred month nor the consecrated gifts not the garlanded animals nor those who are aiming for the sacred house seeking the bounty from their Lord and goodly pleasure. But once you are free from the pilgrimage rituals then hunt and let not the hatred of people incite you to evil doing only because they had barred you from the sacred mosque that you transgress (against them). Nor assist one another unto impiety and unto transgression and revere Allah. Verily Allah is severe in retribution. (The Quran, chapter *The Heavenly Food Bowl,* 5:2)

Also, in chapter *The Night,* they are joined together in this way as expansion—*birr*, and contraction—*taqwa.*

> As for him who gives freely and safeguards his own soul, And believes sincerely in the good promise. We will make it easy for him to find the easy way. But as for him who holds back with stinginess and seeks satisfaction in that which he has, and belies the good promise. We will make easy for him to find the way of hardship. (The Quran, 92:5-10)

FIFTH STATION: ARRIVING AT HOME

It is a normal practice for every traveler to carry with him or her some food, drink or weapon as provision of the way or even as gifts to give upon arrival. Sometimes even he is expected after a long absence to bring home the fruits of his adventure. However, the Merciful God doesn't ask the children to bring with them any goodies as a present. All He wants them to bring is to bring themselves intact and unscathed in their attire of *taqwa. Just come home safe and sound, that's all I want,* He tells them. What do you need to bring to the home of the Most Bounteous when there is everything in abundance? So don't exert yourselves, don't take yourselves beyond the norm. *I don't ask you to bring Me any valuables or any good deeds, as long as you come home with taqwa.* Make *taqwa* your provision, which, if you do, you will arrive home safely. At home you will find every deluxe that you ever thought of and that which you never imagined. But to make it home you must come home attired in your immaculate armour of *taqwa*, for none enters home with a stain on his dress. *All I ask of you is to come Home with no stain on you.* Then you belong home.

> The pilgrimage consists of months well marked so whoever takes upon himself the pilgrimage within these (months), then there should be no obscenity and no acts of renegation and no arguments on pilgrimage. And whatever you do of good, Allah does know it and carry with you your provision of the way. Lo! The best provision of the way indeed is the reverence of Allah and revere Me, O people of the heart. (The Quran, chapter *The Cow*, 2:197)

The fifth station is the final station and the end of the journey for the pilgrim. It is the last stage after which the pilgrim—if he succeeds—is given his rope of honour in which he or she is presented to his Lord, an introduction etiquette exchanging greetings of peace (*salam*) with Him and also with the presence there consisting of the glorious from among whom are the angels, jinns and humans. After this introduction then they are all invited to go and take part in the bridal festivities—the bride is the paradise (*jannah*) and the father of the bride is the Prophet, peace be upon him. For this every glorious soul is introduced twice.

> O you the soul most tranquil! Return to your Lord pleased and pleased with. And enter among My servants. And enter My garden. (The Quran, chapter *The Break of Day*, 89:27-30)

The first introduction is into the presence of the All Mighty and the company of the glorious souls, and the second introduction is into *jannah*, metaphorically known as the bride. The occasion of the wedding festivities is that in which every soul finds its mate at the tune of celestial melodies. They eat whatever their heart may wish and drink the wine of pre-eternity that gives no headache nor causes intoxication. To the accompaniment of those celestial melodies, they dance in pairs with no fatigue or languor.

> He who has made us settle in the home of the everlasting abode from His favour. No toil will touch us therein nor will weariness touch us therein. (The Quran, chapter *Originator of Creation*, 35:35)

This is the scene that follows after the successful completion of the fifth and the final stage. So everything that went before, and everything that comes after, all depend on this final stage. If the pilgrim falls, everything that was done before becomes null and void from the first station until now. This nullification of all the past good deeds is caused mainly by one thing: misconduct and failure to observe the proper manners (*adab*) during the conduct of the rites of Hajj. Yes, it is from that good conduct and observation of proper *adab* required everywhere else wherever the believer maybe for God is with you wherever you are.

> He it is who created the heavens and the earth in six periods and then He established Himself on the throne. He knows what enters into the earth and what comes out of it and what comes down from the heaven and what ascends in it. He is with you wherever you are and Allah is all seeing about whatever you do. (The Quran, chapter *The Iron*, 57:4)

While the ownership of other places is attributed to other than God—they say, this is so and so's house, land, country, or territory—it is only at the *Haram* in Mecca where the title deed is only in God's name. It is consecrated in the name of God, and is known as the Sacred Sanctuary of God, or the House of God. And since it is consecrated only in His name as the sole owner, this portion of earth is the common property of the entire humankind.

> Verily those who disbelieve and hinder people from the way of Allah and from the sacred mosque, which We have made open to all men, the one who dwell therein as well as the one from abroad. But whosoever intends to commit an act of perversion therein by ascribing partners to Allah, We will make him taste from a painful punishment. (The Quran, chapter *The Pilgrimage*, 22:25)

> And when we designated for Abraham the place for the house (and We said to him): do not ascribe anything as a partner to Me, cleanse my house for those who circumambulate and for those who stand steadfast in prayer and for those who bow down and prostrate. (The Quran, chapter *The Pilgrimage*, 22:26)

For this reason God said to Abraham, peace be upon him, *call the human beings,* not just one nation, race, people or tribe. This is the universal call of Abraham and the universal message of Hajj.

> And announce pilgrimage unto mankind they will come to you on foot and on every courser they will come out of every deep narrow path. (The Quran, chapter *The Pilgrimage*, 22:27)

Therefore, since this is the place which has been allocated to God on earth, misconduct here is not like misconduct elsewhere and ill manners here is not like ill manners elsewhere. The consequences are much graver, incurring not only sin but also God's anger. For this reason, God says the best provision to carry with you when you go to this sacred scene is *taqwa*. One must armour himself with *taqwa* all the time, but most imperative at two times: when he goes on pilgrimage to the *Ka'ba* (God's House) in Mecca and when he goes on its heavenly counterpart in the seventh degree of heaven called *bait al-ma'moor*. One pilgrimage takes place during our life on earth and results in our rebirth and our new identity. This one is a preparation and a rehearsal for our second birth at death—the birth of a new soul and a new identity called "the tranquil soul" (*nafs al mutmainna*). Therefore *taqwa*, which means to observe the highest respect and reverence towards God and anything that appertains to God, is the best thing that an itinerant slave needs to take with himself as he goes to meet his Lord.

TAWBAH: THE PILGRIM'S AMENDMENT

All the disciplines that are imposed on the pilgrim, from the first to the fifth station, are meant to prepare him or her thoroughly for that final encounter with his or her Lord. To observe the etiquettes of good conduct (*adab* and *taqwa*) is of the utmost importance once we find ourselves in God's presence. For once we enter this presence, there is no room for making amends or reparations, whereas if we make a mistake or slip at any point during the five stations, we have the opportunity to amend our errors and to repair the damage. This act of reparation or amendment is known as *tawbah*.

The door of *tawbah* is open to you before you die or before you meet God. After death, there is no chance of *tawbah* left. If you fall, you fall for good. Satan (*Iblis*) fell from grace and could never recover after because his is error was lacking of showing respect to God and to His commandment; and to make matters worse, he argued. These are two of the three prohibitions that one must keep away from in Hajj. All three prohibitions include:

1. Professing obscenities, language with sexual content (*rafath*)
2. Acts of disobedience to God's commandments (*fusuq*)

3. Argument (*jidaal*)

Iblis was guilty of two of these offences: 1) he disobeyed God's commandment, and 2) he argued with God—causing him to fall twice and to be cursed twice. He was incapable of recovering after his fall because he continued to argue. But the worst mistake Iblis made was to ask God to grant him to live until to the Day of Ressurection.

> He said, 'O Iblis! What has prevented you from prostrating for that which I have created with my hands? Have you become one of the great ones or are you one of those of high?' He said, 'I am better than him. You created me from fire and You created him from clay.' He said, 'Go out of it, verily you are a pelted one. And verily My curse is on you until the day of the recompense.' He said, 'O my Lord! Then give me respite until the day they shall be raised.' He said, 'So you indeed are among those who are given the respite. Till the day of the appointed time.' He (Iblis) said, 'And by your might, I will surely cause them to stray from the straight path, all of them.' (The Quran, chapter *Sad*, 38:75-81)

The fact that Iblis was not going to die any more sealed his fate because *tawbah* is only open to the mortal and Iblis is immortal. Adam' s chance of recovery was through the recognition of his mortality—had he not recognized his mortality he could never have recovered. The mere recognition of one's mortality is an act of *tawbah*. It brings you to the awareness of God as immortal and ever living.

Once you have the awareness that God is immortal and ever living and that you are mortal and finite, that awareness in turn will lead you to witness the qualities of inadequacy and imperfection in yourself as opposed to the qualities of perfection and adequacy in God. Firstly, He is All-Knowing and you are ignorant; (for how else can a mortal be). There was a time when you did not exist and there is going to be a time when you will not exist. Therefore, how much can you know? Nothing. Secondly, God is All-Powerful and you are weak and powerless. Your weakness and powerlessness is testified by the fact that you sleep and you die, whereas God, who is All-Powerful, All-Mighty, never sleeps nor dies. If you realize this,then you have one of following two options. The first is to repent by surrendering yourself and everything that is yours into the hands of God and ask Him, as The All Living, to dispose of you and yours on your behalf as He sees fit; because He knows and you don't know, and He is capable and you are incapable. This is an act of surrender and repentance (*tawbah*) and reliance (*tawakkul*) at the same time. The second option would be to take your own affairs in your own hands.

> So put your trust on The All Living who dies not and glorify Him along with His praise and sufficient it is that He is all acquainted with the sins of His slaves. (The Quran, chapter *The Criterion*, 25:58)

We can therefore conclude that it is the wishful love for immortality which is the root cause of all deviation, and that the recognition of your mortality is the root cause of all uprightness. It was the love of immortality that caused both Iblis and Adam, peace be upon him, to fall.

> So Satan whispered to him: O Adam may I show you the tree of eternal life and a kingdom that will never decay. (The Quran, chapter *Ta-Ha*, 20:120)

> But the Satan made evil insinuations to both of them so that he may reveal to both of them what was hidden from both of them from their nudeness and he said: your Lord did not forbid you from this tree except that both of you should become angels or that both of you should be of those who live forever. (The Quran, chapter *The Heights*, 7:20)

However, Adam and Eve quickly repented and recognized their mortality, but Iblis persisted by arguing and asking to be made immortal. Therefore, by his own asking, he excluded any chance of recovery and repentance.

CHAPTER 13

The Ornaments of Faith

Faith (*iman*) is likened by God to an essence, a beautiful substance. That essence or beautiful substance is adorned with seven ornamentations.

> [...] but Allah has caused you to love the faith and has adorned it (the faith) in your hearts and He caused you to abhor the disbelief and the renegation and the disobedience. Those are the ones who are well-guided. (The Quran, chapter *The Inner Apartments*, 49:7)

There are two key concepts here: 1. *iman* as act and reality of love; 2. this love of *iman* is in the heart and not outwardly. The word for love is *hubb* and the opposite of love is *kurh* (hate or dislike); for if you love something, perforce you will dislike its opposite. The love of *iman* therefore consists of three things for which there are also three counterparts:

1. Gratitude (*shukr*) and against it ingratitude (*kufr*);
2. Obedience (*ta'a*) and disobedience (*fusuq*); and
3. Remembrance (*dhikr*) and against it forgetfulness (*'isyan*).

Adam's error sprung from forgetfulness; he forgot that he was mortal; while Iblis' error was not forgetfulness but rather a wilful rebellion, disobedience and a wish to be immortal. Adam, peace be upon him, repented and he was accepted back, and Iblis continued on his self-destructive path.

> So Adam received words from His Lord so He turned to him in repentance. Verily He is The Acceptor of Repentance, The Most Merciful. (The Quran, chapter *The Cow*, 2:37)

Therefore love of faith consists of three things:

1. To be grateful to God and not to be ungrateful;
2. To obey God's commandment without question or argument;
3. To remember God and not to forget Him.

If these three things—remembrance, obedience, and gratitude sink down into the heart's core, known as the black spot of the heart, then indeed that person has a love of *iman* in his heart. That means he loves God and His messenger and all his brethren among the messengers, the angels, the books, the hereafter, and destiny as God's will and decision. Equally, he must also abhor their counterparts—ingratitude, disobedience and forgetfulness—and also abhor the enemies of God, His messengers, His angels, His books and so forth. Now love has substantiated in his heart. From being a mere concept, a notion, a perception, it has now become a substance.

Likewise as the foetus becomes a substance in the womb from the fusion of male and female seminal elements, faith turns into a substance in the heart of the faithful. It begins from the drop of the water of life into the heart upon the seed of love. That seed is the good word that lies in the heart, which then springs to full blossom under the effect of the water of life. After the completion of the substantiation of faith in the heart, this final product is known as love.

Following this process is the ornamentation of this love. The ornaments, which are dresses, are both a source of embellishment and protection. As a source of embellishment, it is capable of attracting things that are good and beautiful, and as a source of protection it is capable of repelling things that are harmful and ugly or incongenious. Without these dresses or ornaments, the substance of *iman* in the heart stands exposed to harm or even miscarriage, God forbid. The functions of these ornaments for the substance of *iman* in the heart are similar to the functions of the stars in the heaven. They both adorn the heaven and also repel the intrusion of Satan and his devils.

> And We indeed have adorned the lower heaven with lamps and We have made them missiles to pelt the Satans away and We have readied for them punishment of the blazing fire. (The Quran, chapter *The Dominion*, 67:5)

These dresses or ornaments of *iman* are seven in number—the outer most is white and the inner most is black and in between there are shades of black from yellow to brown to red to blue to green. With white and black at the two ends of the spectrum a process of balanced expansion and contraction sets in. The white is for expansion which has the function to spread and also to repel. The black is for contraction—it is the magnetic core—it attracts and gathers. So between reflection and attraction, and expansion and contraction, the heart is in a tranquil, balanced state (*nafs al mutmainna*). The outermost white dress acts like the white of the pupil of the eye in relation to the retina which is one of the shades of black, blue, etc. It is also like the hard white shell of an egg as opposed to the yolk inside which is yellow. This white protective dress is known as the dress of *taqwa*. Its white color has dual functions. The first is to help reflect light and also deflect harm. The second is to be detect easily if there is a stain so that one may quickly remove the stain and keep other stains away.

There are seven ornaments of *iman* which are all a protection and a decoration for *iman*. They correspond to the seven layers of the seven heavens. These seven ornaments can be grouped under the title of "Ornaments of Love."

The FIRST ornament of love is called *taqwa*:

God says that He loves those who characteristically have *taqwa* as their dress.

> O children of Adam! We indeed have sent down upon you garments which covers your nudity and as ornamentation and yet the garment of God's reverence, that is the best. That is of the signs of Allah so that they may oft-remember. (The Quran, chapter *The Heights,* 7:26)

> Nay! Indeed whoever fulfills his firm pledge and safeguards his own soul, then verily Allah loves those who safeguard their own souls. (The Quran, chapter *The Family of Imran,* 3:76)

> Except those whom you have made covenant with from among those who ascribe partners to Allah and thereafter they have not cheated you anything in the least and they have not backed anyone against you so fulfill the covenant for them until its term. Verily Allah loves those who guard their own souls. (The Quran, chapter *The Repentance*, 9:4)

> How could there be any covenant in the sight of Allah and in the sight of His messenger for those who ascribe partners to Allah except the ones with whom you have made the covenant in the precinct of the sacred mosque. Therefore as long as they observe their duty to you, then do observe your duty to them. Verily Allah loves those who safeguard their own souls. (The Quran, chapter *The Repentance*, 9:7)

The SECOND ornament of love is *tawbah*:

> And they ask you (O Muhammad) about the monthly

cycle. Say: it is a temporary discomfiture therefore keep away from women in their monthly cycle and do not come near unto them until they are cleansed and when they are cleansed then approach them from whence Allah has commanded you. Verily Allah loves those who oft repent and He loves those who purify themselves" (The Quran, chapter *The Cow* 2:222)

The THIRD ornament of love is *tahara*:

> And they ask you (O Muhammad) about the monthly cycle. Say: it is a temporary discomfiture therefore keep away from women in their monthly cycle and do not come near unto them until they are cleansed and when they are cleansed then approach them from whence Allah has commanded you. Verily Allah loves those who oft repent and He loves those who purify themselves. (The Quran, chapter *The Cow*, 2:222)

> Do not stand therein (for prayer) ever. Surely a mosque which was founded on the reverence of God from the first day has more right for you to stand therein (for prayer). Therein are men who love to purify themselves and Allah loves those who purify themselves. (The Quran, chapter *The Repentance,* 9:108)

The FOURTH ornament of love is *ihsan*:

> Those who spend in the time of ease and in the time of hardship and those who keep in check the rage and those who pardon the people and Allah loves those who act in excellence. (The Quran, chapter *The Family of Imran*, 3:134)

> Because of their violation of their solemn covenant, We cursed them and We made their hearts hard. They bias the word from its rightful disposition and they forgot a

> share from that which was given to them as a reminder and you will continue to discover treachery from them except a few among them but pardon them and turn away in a nicely way. Verily Allah loves those who act in excellence. (The Quran, chapter *The Heavenly Food Bowl*, 5:13)

> So Allah gave them reward of this world and an excellent reward of the hereafter and Allah loves those who act in excellence. (The Quran, chapter *The Family of Imran*, 3:148)

The FIFTH ornament of love is *tawakkul*:

> Indeed it is due to a mercy from Allah that you are lenient to them; if you were furious and hard hearted, then they would have surely scattered away from around you. Therefore pardon them; and ask forgiveness for them and give them share in the command. But when you make up your mind then put your trust on Allah. Verily Allah loves those who put their trust in Him. (The Quran, chapter *The Family of Imran* 3:159)

The SIXTH ornament of love is *qist*:

> And when two groups from the believers fight among themselves then reconcile between them; and if one of the two is belligerent against the other then fight against the one who is belligerent until he turns back (complies) to the commandment of Allah. But when it [the belligerent group] does turn back then reconcile between them in justice and be fair. Verily Allah loves those who are equitable. (The Quran, chapter *The Inner Apartements*, 49:9)

> Allah does not bar you from those who have not fought against you in the religion and who have not driven you out of your homes that you be kind to them and that you

> treat them with equity. Verily Allah loves those who are equitable. (The Quran, chapter *The Woman Tried in Faith*, 60:8)

> Often listening to the lie, often devouring the illicit gains. So if they come to you then arbitrate between them or turn away from them; and if you turn away from them then they will never harm you in aught but if you arbitrate between them then arbitrate between them with uprightness. Verily Allah loves those who are equitable. (The Quran, chapter *The Heavenly Food Bowl*, 5:42)

The SEVENTH ornament of love is *sabr*:

> And how many a prophet who fought (in the way of Allah) with him were many Godly men but they did not get faint at heart for what happened to them in the way of Allah nor did they get weak nor did they succumb and Allah loves those who are patient. (The Quran, chapter *The Family of Imran*, 3:146)

These seven virtuous ornaments help consolidate the tender sprout of love and turn it into a permanent feature of your character. In sum, they are:

TAQWA is reverence or respect for God or what appertains to God—like His Signs and His creations. This reverence contributes to safeguarding our soul by preventing them from transgression.

TAWBAH is recognition of your shortcomings and corresponding recognition of God's mercy and forgiveness and therefore reverting to Him each time you err for forgiveness, pardon and blessing

TAHARA is to love to cultivate purity in words, in heart, in mind, in body, in food and drink, etc. Part of this is usage of water for cleaning and respecting women in the menstrual blood.

IHSAN is to be charitable in all circumstances—to initiate giving and to return good for good and to return good for wrong.

TAWAKKUL is reliance on God or to delegate your affairs and allow God to act on your behalf instead of taking it in your own hands. It is to trust God with yourself and whatever is yours to God.

QIST is uprightness, to be equitable, just, and fair in dealing with those whom you love and those whom you don't love, with friend and foe alike.

SABR is patience and steadfastness, it is a quality of persistence in the pursuit of truth regardless of harm or obstruction. Three conditions must prevail for you to have *sabr*: a) not to give in; b) not to feel low in morale or dispirited; c) and not to be subdued nor be sheepish.

These seven ornaments of love correspond to the seven degrees of the soul. The believer is invested with one of these gowns each time he mounts a degree. These seven ornaments of love also have the substance of faith making them eight altogether. This eight corresponds to the eight degrees of paradise.

Corresponding to these seven ornamental dresses of faith are the seven ornamental dresses of disbelief. As faith in substance is made up of shukr (*gratitude*), obedience (*ta'ah*), and remembrance (*dhikr*); the counterpart of faith is made up of three things: ingratitude (*kufr*), disobedience (*fusuq*), and forgetfulness (*'isyan*). If these three penetrate into the heart until they are substantiated, they turn into love of everything that is counter to faith and hate of everything that is of faith. It attracts what is harmful and ugly, and repels what is good and beautiful. It becomes an inverted heart, it gets all the values inverted—the ugly looks beautiful, the stenchy smells fragrant, charity looks ignorant, and stinginess appears intelligent. In sum, all the values are upside down as opposed to the upright heart of the faithful.

> Is the one whose evil deed is made to look goodly in his eyes so that he sees it as an excellent deed [equal to the one who is well guided by Allah]? Verily Allah allows to go astray whom He pleases and guides whom He pleases so do not let your soul grieve over them. Verily Allah is all knowing about all that they fabricate. (The Quran, chapter *Originator of Creation*, 35:9)

> Is one who is on a clear proof from his Lord like one to whom his evil deeds have been made seemly to him and so they followed their vain desires. (The Quran, chapter *Muhammad*, 47:14)

> And do not insult those they invoke besides Allah then they will insult Allah out of transgression without knowledge. Thus We have made seemly to every nation their deeds and then unto their Lord is their place of return and then He will inform them about all that they used to do. (The Quran, chapter *the Cattle*, 6:108)

The Prophet, peace be upon him, has divided the hearts into three kinds: a heart that is cleared, bright and levelled like a burning lamp in it; a heart that is upside down; and a heart which that is twisted. The first kind is the heart of a faithful believer and the burning lamp is the light (*noor*) of his *iman*. The second is the heart of a disbeliever whose heart is turned upside down. Their upside down heart perceives things invertedly—the negative as positive, the short as tall, the white as black, the east as west, and miserliness as charity. The third, which is the twisted heart, is the heart of a hypocrite. It is twisted because his heart fluctuates between both sides—between faith and disbelief. One part of his heart is diseased and the other part is healthy, and whichever side that dominates will determine his fate.

Now it remains to specify the opposites of these seven ornaments of love, for is not enough to only know what is good; it is also important to know what is wrong so as to avoid it. Since faith is an essence, meaning, it has a substantial reality; non-faith is neither essence and has no substantial reality. It is the mere absence of faith. Therefore it is a nothingness, a mere shadow, a mirage, an illusion or imagination.

> And those who disbelieve, their deeds are like a mirage in a desert which the thirsty takes to be water until when he comes to it, he does not find it to be anything but he finds Allah with him thereupon He gives him his reckoning in full and Allah is swift in the reckoning. (The Quran, chapter *The Light*, 24:39)

> There are but names you have coined, you and your fathers. Allah has not sent down any authority by them. They but follow the wishful thinking and that which the souls desire, and the guidance has indeed come unto them from their Lord. (The Quran, chapter *The Star*, 53:23)

> Have you seen him who has taken his vain desires as his god? Are you then going to be a trustee over him. (The Quran, chapter *The Criterion*, 25:43)

It cannot be otherwise, for the true existence only belongs to God, and to believe in God makes the believer part of that true existence. Therefore, if only God truly exists, everything else besides God has no true existence. Thus to not believe in God is to believe in nothing, likewise to believe in something other than God is also to believe in nothing. So those who don't believe in God or those who believe in something other than God all end up in nothing, with nothing, and not-being. If being is life and not being is non-life, therefore to believe in God is to believe in life and not to believe in God is to deny to be and to live. The differences between the living and the dead is that the living can hear *and* respond to what he hears: he can also speak. And so, the definition of a full living being is that it can hear, understand, and respond, meaning, it is capable of communicating. If it hears for example, but cannot respond, then it is not considered a full living being. Responding depends on understanding, so even though someone may hear, he or she may not be able to understand, and one who fails to understand, cannot respond.

> Only they who hear can respond and as for the dead, Allah will raise them and then unto Him they will be brought back. (The Quran, chapter *The Cattle,* 6:36)

> So that We may revive a dead land with it and that We cause to drink from it many of those that We have created: cattle and human beings. (The Quran, chapter *The Criterion*, 25:49)

> Verily you cannot make the dead hear nor can you make the deaf hear the call when they have turned their backs away. (The Quran, chapter *The Romans,* 30:52)

Humans are faced with two kinds of deafness: one that can hear but cannot understand nor is able to respond, and the one who doesn't even hear, that is, the complete deaf. While sight constitutes a later stage of life, the foundation is the hearing, since it is through the hearing that a communication is established. God initiates the process—He calls and we respond, and then we call and He responds, and in this way a dialogue is established between Creator and created.

Therefore life and death is not in terms of flesh and blood—we share that with the animals—it is in terms of hearing and understanding and then responding.

> So he brought forth for them a calf with a body and it has a bellowing sound, so they said: this is your god and the

> God of Moses, but he (Samiri) forgot. Do they not see that it does not speak back to them a word and does not control any harm or any benefit for them. (The Quran, chapter *Ta-Ha,* 20:88-89)

Until someone is able to hear from God, to understand His message, and to respond to His communication, he or she is not counted among the living. If you listen to the recital of the revealed word of God, it is as though you have heard from God; if you understand it therefore you have understood the message of God; and if you respond to it then you have fulfilled all conditions of a living being—to hear, to understand and to respond. This response is called obedience, for the message must contain a commandment: what to do, or what not to do, or when or how to do something. God has sent no messengers nor revealed books of law to the animals because even though they can hear, they cannot understand, and consequently cannot respond either in the affirmative or in the negative. The mentally handicapped or children underage are also exempted from the commands of the law because they lack the understanding and the ability to respond.

Therefore, the definition of a living being is the one who hears or sees and understands what he hears, and responds appropriately to the message.

> And when the Quran is recited, do listen to it and be silent so that perhaps you may receive mercy. (The Quran, chapter *The Height,* 7:204)

> And if My servants ask you about Me then know that I am indeed close. I answer the call of the caller if he calls Me. Therefore, let them respond to Me and let them believe in Me perhaps they will find the right guidance. (The Quran, chapter *The Cow,* 2:186)

> If you call them they do not hear your call and even if

> they hear, they cannot answer you and on the day of resurrection they will deny your making them as partners with Allah and none can inform you like one who is all acquainted. (The Quran, chapter *Originator of Creation*, 35:14)

> And who is more misguided than one who calls besides Allah such a one who will not respond back to him till the day of resurrection while they (the gods) are completely oblivious about their invocation. (The Quran, chapter *The Winding Sand Tracts*, 46:5)

> Verily those that you call besides Allah are slaves like unto you so call them and let them respond to you if you indeed are veridical. (The Quran, chapter *The Heights*, 7:194)

These verses signify that only He is worthy of calling upon and worthy of being supplicated, because He can hear and He knows your intent and He is capable of responding. Those who call on anything besides Him are calling nothing and nothing has neither hearing, understanding nor the power to respond. So call upon Him if you believe that only He is, but when you call Him, call Him as though you see Him, that is, He is with you and close to you. If you call Him as something that is not with you and that is far from you, then you are calling on nothing. So He is with you and He is close to you. His proximity is not a physical proximity nor is His being with you a physical company. It is in terms of closeness of hearing, seeing and understanding.

> He said: Do not fear both of you for verily I am with both of you and I hear and I see. (The Quran, chapter *Ta-Ha*, 20:46)

> Say: If I am misguided, then my misguidance is only against my own soul but if I am guided it is because of

> what my Lord has revealed unto me. Verily He is All Hearing, All Near. (The Quran, chapter *The Kingdom of Saba*, 34:50)

> He it is who created the heavens and the earth in six periods and then He established Himself on the throne. He knows what enters into the earth and what comes out of it and what comes down from the heaven and what ascends in it. He is with you wherever you are and Allah is all seeing about whatever you do. (The Quran, chapter *The Iron*, 57:4)

Progressively, the slave gets nearer and nearer to God by listening to Him, understanding His speech and acting upon it, until a total union takes place between the slave and the Master. Such that sight fuses with sight, hearing fuses with hearing and understanding with understanding. So closeness to God is not a physical nearness—it is only in terms of hearing, seeing, understanding and responding. The prophet, peace be upon him said:

> Allah said: '[...] My slave approaches Me with nothing more beloved to Me than what I have made obligatory upon him, and My slave keeps drawing nearer to Me with voluntary works until I love him. And when I love him, I am his hearing with which he hears, his sight with which he sees, his hand with which he seizes, and his foot with which he walks. If he asks me, I will surely give to him, and if he seeks refuge in Me, I will surely protect him.' (*Hadith Qudsi*)

This transformation and the adaptation of these qualities of the slave to the qualities of the Master announces the beginning of a union of love between the two. That union has seven degrees, known as the degrees of love or the ornaments of faith (*iman*).

Conversely, non-faith in Allah means belief in nothing, because only things are that hear, understand and respond and only God per excellence hears, understands and responds. Those who have experienced union with Him also hear but by or with Him, they understand with or by Him, and they respond with or by Him. Those who are not part of this union do not hear, understand nor respond, and are counted as dead and part of the nothing. Belief in this "nothing" also breeds seven kinds of inverted love. Each one corresponds to one of the seven degrees of Hell, the abode of nothingness. The love of nothingness is also called love of lust, as opposed to the love of faith which is love of God. If this love of lust settles in the heart, it breeds seven characteristics of the soul, each being an opposite of the seven loves of *iman*.

> Love of the lusts has been made seemly unto mankind from the women and the children and the amassed treasures of gold and silver and the horses of high breed and the cattle and the farm. That is the temporary pleasure of the life of this world. But Allah, indeed with Him is the excellent place of return. (The Quran, chapter *The Family of Imran*, 3:14)

The love of lust in the heart therefore breeds the following vices:

1. '*Udwan* or *fujoor* (transgression) as opposed to *taqwa*:

> O you who believe! Do not violate the rights of Allah nor the sacred month nor the consecrated gifts nor the garlanded animals nor those who are aiming for the sacred house seeking the bounty from their Lord and goodly pleasure. But once you are free from the pilgrimage rituals then hunt and let not the hatred of people incite you to evil doing only because they had barred you from the sacred mosque that you transgress (against them). And assist one another unto the piety and unto Allah's reverence and do not assist one another unto impiety and unto

transgression and revere Allah. Verily Allah is severe in retribution. (The Quran, chapter *The Heavenly Food Bowl*, 5:2)

O you who believe! Do not make unlawful the good things that Allah has made lawful for you but do not transgress. Verily Allah loves not those who are transgressors. (The Quran, chapter *The Heavenly Food Bowl*, 5:87)

And by a soul and how He extended its creation. And then He inspired it to know its transgression and its self-guard. (The Quran, chapter *The Sun*, 91:7-8)

Invoke your Lord clamorously and silently. He indeed does not love the transgressors. (The Quran, chapter *The Heights*, 7:55)

2. *Israaf* (extravagance) as opposed to *qist*:

He it is who has raised the gardens; ones which are husbanded and ones which are not husbanded and the date-palms and the crops of various tastes and the olive and the pomegranate similar to one another and dissimilar ones. Eat from its fruit when it has fructified and give out its due on the day of its harvest and do not be extravagant. Verily He loves not those who are extravagant. (The Quran, chapter *The Cattle*, 6:141)

3. *Dhulm* (wrongfulness) as opposed to *ihsan*:

And the price for ill is ill like unto it, but one who pardons and amends, indeed his reward is upon Allah. Verily He does not love the wrongdoers. (The Quran, chapter *The Consultation*, 42:40)

And as for those who believe and work the righteous deeds, He will surely give them their reward in full for

Allah loves not those who wrong their own souls. (The Quran, chapter *The Family of Imran*, 3:57)

If pain touches you, then indeed pain touched the people like unto it. And those days We rotate between people and so that Allah may mark out those who believe and that He may take out the witnesses from among you and Allah loves not those who wrong their own souls. (The Quran, chapter *the Family of Imran*, 3:140)

4. *Ifsad* (corruption) as opposed to *sabr*:

And the Jews say: Allah's hand is tied. Their hands are tied and they are cursed for what they say. Nay! Both His hands are wide open. He spends whichever way He pleases but that which has been sent down to you from your Lord will surely increase many of them in transgression and in disbelief and We have given rise between them to enmity and rancour till the day of the resurrection. Whenever they kindle a fire for war, Allah extinguishes it and they strive in the earth spreading corruption and Allah does not love those who spread corruption. (The Quran, chapter *The Heavenly Food Bowl*, 5:64)

And seek the home of the hereafter out of that which Allah has bestowed on you but forget not your share from the life of this world. And be good (unto others) as Allah has been good unto you and seek not the corruption in the earth for truly Allah loves not the corruptors. (The Quran, chapter *The Stories*, 28:77)

5. *Istikabaar* (arrogance) as opposed to *tawbah*.

It is no wonder that Allah does know all that they conceal and all that they reveal. Verily, He does not love those who continue to be arrogant. (The Quran, chapter *The Bee*, 16:23)

6. *Khiyana* (treachery) as opposed to *tahara*:

> And if you ever fear betrayal on the part of any people, then cast back on them their covenant to be on equal terms. Verily Allah does not love the traitors. (The Quran, chapter *The Gains of War,* 8:58)

> And do not argue on behalf of those who cheat their own selves. Verily Allah does not love whoever is indeed treacherous and sinful. (The Quran, chapter *The Women,* 4:107)

> Verily Allah defends those who believe. Verily Allah loves not anyone who is treacherous, ungrateful. (The Quran, chapter *The Pilgrimage,* 22:38)

7. *Farah* (exultation) as opposed to *tawakkul*:

> Lo! Qarun was of the people of Moses but he trespassed upon them and We did give him from treasures such that the keys thereof will weigh heavy on a band of strong men. When his people said unto him: do not exult. For truly Allah loves not those who are exultant. (The Quran, chapter *The Stories*, 28:76)

> And do not turn your cheek arrogantly to men and do not walk in the earth exultantly, verily Allah does not love any self-conceited and self-vaunting. (The Quran, chapter *Luqman,* 31:18)

> So that you do not grieve over that which you fail to attain nor exult over that which you have achieved and Allah does not love any who is self-conceited, self-vaunting. (The Quran, chapter *The Iron,* 57:23)

> And serve Allah and do not ascribe anything as a partner

> to Him, and show kindness to the parents and to the near of kin and to the orphans and to the needy ones and to the neighbour who is near of kin and to the neighbour who is not a blood relation and to the companion who lives by your side and to the wayfarer and to those that your right hand possess. Verily Allah does not love anyone who is indeed self-conceited and boastful. (The Quran, chapter *The Women,* 4:36)

These are the seven branches that have grown on the tree of disbelief (*kufr*). This tree is from the evil seed which is the evil word of denial (*kalimatul kufr*) as opposed to the tree of *iman* which is the tree from the good seed which in turn is the good word, the word of faith, the affirmative word.

> Bringing forth its fruit in every season by the permission of its Lord and Allah sets parables for human beings so that they may remember. And the likeness of an evil word is like that of an evil tree which is uprooted unto the surface of the earth having no place to settle in. (The Quran, chapter *Abraham,* 14:25-26)

> Whoever is seeking the might, verily all the might is for Allah. To Him mounts up the good word and the good deed: He raises it up. And those who are scheming the evil deeds, for them is a formidable punishment and the scheme of this, it is this that is going to waste. (The Quran, chapter *Originator of Creation*, 35:10)

THE EVIL WORD

The evil word consists of denial that there is no God, there is no truth and nothing has been revealed from God—it is a series of doubt, scepticism and denial. This is the evil word—it is the word of nothingness.

> They said: you are but human beings like us and The All

> Merciful has sent down nothing of the sort. You are but lying. (The Quran, chapter *Ya-Sin*, 36:15)

> And they have not estimated Allah to His true estimate. When they said: Allah sent nothing to any man. Say: who sent down the book which was brought by Moses as a light and guidance for mankind. You make it into booklets you show parts of it and you hide most; and you were taught which you knew not nor did your fathers say: Allah. Then forsake them diving in their idleness and playing. (The Quran, chapter *The Cattle*, 6:91)

> And whenever it is said to them: what is it that your Lord has revealed. They say: tales of the ancient. (The Quran, chapter *The Bee*, 16:24)

> Their hearts are idle and those who have wronged their own souls hold a secret counsel among themselves saying: Is this anything but a mortal like you? Will you then yield to magic while you see plainly. (The Quran, chapter *The Prophets*, 21:3)

> And when it is said unto them: believe the way everyone has believed. They say: should we believe the way the simpletons have believed? Nay indeed it is they who are the simpletons but they know not. (The Quran, chapter *The Cow*, 2:13)

As you can see through these verses are all about denial, denial of everything.

THE GOOD WORD

As for the good word, it is about faith, trust and positiveness. It consists of denying everything and affirming only one: Allah! So the statement *"la ilaha illa Allah"*—the negative *"la ilaha"* (there is no diety) is a sweeping act meant to purify the heart from everything or from all things except (*illa)* one thing—*Allah*. That means everything except Allah is nothing. The statement of witnessing is four words:

la—ilaha—illa—Allah

only the last word (*Allah*) is a confirmation and the three preceding words are purificational negation. That purificational negation is an expansion meant to sweep away and cleanse the heart to become the contraction and confirmation of the word *Allah*. For this reason many teachers just teach their disciples to say "*Allah*" without the negation. It is the affirmation of the unity of God, meaning unity of essence. It is the one word, that is the word of faith, opposing the many words which are the words of *kufr*. Nothingness and manyness are correlates as being and unity are also correlates. For this reason God says to the Prophet, peace be upon him, that if you see them indulging in speculations or entertaining so many words, say "*Allah!*" And let them indulge in their vain talk.

> Say: which thing is greater in witnessing? Say: Allah; He is a witness between me and you and this Quran has been revealed to me so that I may warn you thereby and anyone that it may reach. Will you indeed bear witness that there are other deities besides Allah? Say: as for me I do not witness. Say: He is but one deity and I indeed disavow all that you ascribe as partners to Him. (The Quran, chapter *The Cattle,* 6:19)

> And they have not estimated Allah to His true estimate. When they said: Allah sent nothing to any man. Say: who sent down the book which was brought by Moses as a light and guidance for mankind. You make it into booklets you show parts of it and you hide most and you were taught which you knew not nor did your fathers say 'Allah'. Then forsake them diving in their idleness and playing. (The Quran, chapter *The Cattle,* 6:91)

This word "*Allah*" is the supreme word, superior over every word, and yet the disbelievers cannot stand this word.

> And when Allah all alone is mentioned, the hearts of those who do not believe in the hereafter feel repugnant but when those besides Him (whom they have taken as partners) are mentioned lo! They are filled with joy. (The Quran, chapter *The Flocks,* 39:45)

> If you do not help him then Allah did help him when those who disbelieved drove him out two of the two as the two were in the cave and when he said to his companion: grieve not verily Allah is with us. Thereupon Allah sent down His Sakeena upon him and strengthened him with hosts that you did not see and He made the word of those who disbelieve the lower and the word of Allah that is the higher, and Allah is All Mighty All Wise. (The Quran, chapter *The Repentance,* 9:40)

> Since those who disbelieved put in their hearts the passionate zeal, passionate zeal of the ignorance but Allah sent down tranquility upon His messenger and upon the believers and caused them to abide by the word of *taqwa* 'God Reverence' and they were most entitled to it and they were its kinfolk and verily Allah is all knowing about everything. (The Quran, chapter *The Victory,* 48:26)

In chapter *Ta-Ha,* God relates the secret discussion happening among the resurrected as they wondered how many periods they lasted in the world (*dunya*) or how long their waiting period was. They say ten, ten meaning many. But God says that "The one among them who belonged to the most upright way says: 'You lasted only one day'." It is this oneness that must be perceived through everything.

> Whispering among themselves (some say): you have not tarried in the world but ten days. It is We who know well about what they say when the one among them who is

> best in position says: you have tarried (in the world) but one day. (The Quran, chapter *Ta-Ha,* 20:103-104)

Here, in this story we see the opposition between the "one" and "the many," and the Almighty Himself declares that the one who says "one day" is on the best course. The reason here being that those who affirm "ten"—the manyness—their affirmation implies recognition of being to others besides the One Allah. While the one who affirms "one"—the unity—denies everything else except One. That is the same thing that God tells the Prophet, peace be upon him, to say only "*Allah*" when they indulge in manyness.

The course adopted by the one who considers all days of God as one from beginning to end and from start to last is the best course. This course of thinking is qualified by God Himself as the best course. There are so many paths, but this one is the most sublime, and at the same time the most simple and the most easy. Since One is the beginning and One is at the end, whatever many is in between doesn't count for much; for what matters is the end and the beginning. The end and the beginning are the same, so there is One.

> Say: 'He is Allah the One and Unique, Allah The All Absolute, He begot not nor was He begotten, And there is no equal to Him one and Unique.' (The Quran, chapter *Purity*, 112:1-4)

This is why the name chapter *Purity* (*ikhlas*), came to be named: meaning purity of unity. It begins with "one" (*ahad*), the one and absolute, and ends with one "*ahad*" and what is in between are all negations. There are three negations: "He begot none" (*lam yalid*); "nor was He begotten" (*wa lam yoolad*); "there is no equal to him, One and Unique" (*wa lam yakun lahu kufuwan ahad*), meaning spouse, for your spouse is your equal partner. Interestingly, however, it is these three negations that veil most people from realizing the unity. It is either children, or parents or compeers. This manyness results from four illusions: the illusion of numbers, of colours, of tongues, and of functions. The differentiations and differences as we see in creation all go back to these considerations and only the blessed—those who perceive with the eye of unity (*ahadiyah*)—are saved from the shattering effect of their differences.

> Had your Lord so willed He would indeed have made mankind one nation but however they continue to disagree. Except those on whom your Lord has bestowed His mercy. For that end He created them (to disagree) and your Lord's sentence has been fulfilled that I indeed will fill hell with jinn and human beings altogether. (The Quran, chapter *Hud,* 11:118-119)

> And verily one nation is this your nation and I am your Lord so revere Me. (The Quran, chapter *The Believers,* 23:52)

> Verily this is your nation which is one nation and I am your Lord so serve Me alone. (The Quran, chapter *The Prophets*, 21:92)

Printed in Great Britain
by Amazon